Book selection

Principles and practice

Fifth edition

Book selection

Principles and practice

Fifth edition

David Spiller MLS ALA

With an introduction by Brian Baumfield

LIBRARY ASSOCIATION PUBLISHING
LONDON

A CLIVE BINGLEY BOOK

Published by
Library Association Publishing Ltd
7 Ridgmount Street
London WC1E 7AE

First published 1971
Second edition 1974
Third edition 1980
Fourth edition 1986
This edition 1991

British Library Cataloguing in Publication Data

Spiller, David
    Book selection: principles and practice. — 5th ed.
    I. Title
    025.2

ISBN 0-85157-464-5

Typeset in 11/12pt Baskerville by Library Association Publishing Ltd.
Printed and made in Great Britain by Billing and Sons Ltd, Worcester.

Contents

'You may say that one doesn't really need to read every single book. My retort to that is – in warfare, too, one doesn't need to kill every single soldier, and yet every single one is necessary. Now you will say every single book is necessary too. But there you are, you see, even *there* there's something wrong. For it isn't true. I asked the librarian!'

Robert Musil *The man without qualities*

Introduction

An introduction to what has become the standard work on book selection seems almost superfluous – the fact that it is now in its fifth edition speaks for itself.

Unlike many new editions, there is no question of just a few minor changes but a substantial updating has been undertaken, which will guarantee the student accurate information and guidance in what is generally considered to be the most professional aspect of the practice of librarianship. The definition of what constitutes a profession is one where principles are applied to practice. This book amply demonstrates the validity of such a tenet, and whilst principles in the art of book selection do not change, the practice certainly does. Growth in bibliographical control expands every year through the use of new technology and the ubiquitous computer – it also throws a considerable burden on the selector to master the new tools at his or her disposal. Here then is a guide which will enable this to be achieved.

This new edition has been split into three parts – fundamentals, background and special materials. This will help readers to grasp the complexities and range of the subject more easily. The work is a little shorter in length than the last edition, in order to streamline it, and almost half the text has been rewritten – including the chapters on policy, users, book evaluation and fiction. There is a brief new section on biography, and inevitably more on automation. There are, too, more than one hundred references to new literature.

These are the bare bones of what is to be found in this new edition. To find more the book must be read and studied – as it surely will be. I wish it every success.

Brian Baumfield

Acknowledgement

I would like warmly to thank Brian Baumfield for sharing with me his wide knowledge of the subject of book selection. He has been a mentor for all the editions of this book, and has also contributed a typically generous introduction to the present edition.

David Spiller

Part I

Fundamentals

1 *Definitions*

Terminology in the subject under review is by no means generally agreed upon or consistently applied. The following notes describe how terms are used in this book, and give any alternative uses that have some currency.

Book provision An umbrella term covering a number of activities relating to library stock, including selection, revision, weeding, promotion and interlending.

Collection development A new term originating in the North American academic library sector. It refers to the systematic building up of library collections.

Selection Evaluating and choosing materials to add to library stock.

Weeding Removal of stock from library shelves, either for withdrawal, or for moving to reserve stock or remote storage (when it is known as 'relegation'). See Chapter 11 for other definitions in this area.

Stock revision In-depth revision of stock, taking one subject at a time. It involves examining and weeding existing stock on a subject and studying the pattern of use, then identifying and selecting the most appropriate works in print from the subject bibliography. Sometimes also referred to as **stock editing.**

Stock logistics The quantitative aspects of book provision. These include study of the number of readers and the distribution of their interests as expressed in use of the stock, and analysis

3

of the number of additions required in each subject to ensure sufficient choice of stock. Sometimes also described as **stock analysis** or **systematic bookstock management.**

Acquisition This term is used in two different ways. In this book 'acquisition' is treated simply as a technical process for obtaining materials, following the selection process. A list of duties which can be included in the job specification of an acquisitions department was given in Stephen Ford's excellent monograph *The acquisition of library materials* (2nd edition by R. M. Magrill)[262] as follows: 'maintain ordering tools (bibliographies, publishers' catalogues); maintain order files; perform pre-order bibliographical searching; select booksellers; receive packages of new books; approve invoices; accession new books; supervise subscriptions and standing orders; send booksellers' chasers; search for out-of-print materials.' These duties are markedly different from those involved in selecting, revising or weeding stock, and in most libraries are carried out by different (often non-professional) staff. In the sense just described acquisition procedures are not covered by this book, except in a few instances where 'selection' and 'acquisition' are hard to separate (for example, in the area of secondhand books).

However, some writers – particularly from the academic sector – use the term 'acquisition' in a much broader sense, to cover the whole area of book provision, in addition to the process of obtaining books described immediately above. There is some logic to this, for in a specialized field much of the meaningful work in obtaining books is related to tracing recondite materials, rather than making the selection decision, so that the lines between 'selection' and 'acquisition' become blurred. For the purposes of literature searching it means that the reader cannot on the face of it ignore literature referring to acquisition, since it may well relate also to the selection process.

4

2 The need for effective book provision

It is often said that library and information science is not a subject in itself but a collection of related subjects drawn from other disciplines. The profession's perception of that collection of subjects has changed dramatically in size and scope during the past 20 years, and now takes in developments from computer science, the social sciences, management and many other areas. Nevertheless there remains the valid concept of a core of professional activities which distinguish library and information work from other occupations, and with which most practitioners working from a library service point will be involved on a day-to-day basis.

Provision is one of these core activities. It is concerned with selecting and maintaining the library's resources (books, periodicals, audiovisual materials, electronic media, etc.). The other core activities are arranging the resources (classification and indexing) and using them (reference work, current awareness services, etc.). It may be seen that these three activities must take place in the sequence given above, with selection necessarily coming first, and to that extent it can be argued that provison is the most fundamental of all library activities, with the others depending upon its effective execution. A sophisticated system of information retrieval is of no use unless it affords access to the right documents. Highly trained information staff cannot be effective if they are not using the right resources. An elegant library building becomes a white elephant unless it houses material appropriate for its users. And so on.

This seems self-evident, and yet recent years have been characterized by an extraordinary lack of interest in researching and developing methods of book provision. The climate of apathy extends to library practice, library education, literature and research. To an extent this impression of neglect may be a matter

5

of perception. The provision of materials is in fact a recurring theme of most professional activity. But as noted above, library and information science is an amalgam of disparate disciplines. At present the profession seems loathe to examine those disciplines in terms of their end-products – of which book provision is a fundamental example. Ironically, supporting activities such as management or automation seem all too often to have been developed as end-products in themselves.

In library education, most courses on book provision – if they exist at all – are short, low-profile affairs. In haste to graft on to their syllabuses more prestigious-sounding peripheral subjects, many library schools have signally failed to clarify for their students the fundamental objectives of library service. But without a genuine understanding of fundamentals the student may fail to relate techniques to overall purpose. For all the emphasis on techniques, those relating to book provision – weeding, stock logistics, selection – are rarely taught in any detail.

In the literature, too, works written from a book provision viewpoint are unaccountably sparse, particularly in the key areas of selection and stock revision (whilst, curiously, the literature on weeding and relegation is quite substantial). Little research work is directed towards the needs of book provision, although a long list of worthwhile projects could be suggested. Even in automation areas, where research projects abound, and where there are obvious applications for book provision, few proposals are put forward.

The widespread neglect of such a key subject seems illogical when seen against the broader background – a period during which more books and other materials are being published, at increasing prices, whilst bookfunds in nearly all public and educational library sectors are being cut back. In such circumstances the need for a re-evaluation of provision policies and methods to make best use of limited funding is self-evident – particularly so where libraries have also suffered staffing cuts, and where users are therefore more reliant upon a self-service approach from stock on open shelves.

It is reasonable to ask whether book provision will remain a subject of major importance, in view of the rapid developments now taking place in computerized information systems. No one knows the extent to which traditional materials of communication

6

will be replaced by computerized systems, though everyone has fun guessing. At present, printed materials are by far the most common source of information in most types of library, and within the foreseeable future they are likely to remain so for certain purposes (recreational, cultural and educational reading, as well as for many forms of reading for information). The techniques required for the effective provision of printed material will therefore remain an essential part of the librarian's professional equipment – particularly so in the public library sector.

Nevertheless, in all kinds of library there will be considerable developments in the formats available to libraries for providing information, and in specialized research libraries – where book provision is already of limited importance – the kinds of material used for information provision will change radically. As use of computerized systems increases, the need for librarians to actually possess materials is likely to diminish – although the recent success of the CD-ROM medium shows that there can be no confident predictions in this area. But certainly, databases will continue to proliferate for the foreseeable future, and will become an important component of the services offered as a matter of course by a variety of different kinds of library.

However – and this is the key point – as the number of databases increases, so too will the need to evaluate their content and format in order to select between them (and to select between electronic and printed formats of the same product, since they very often run alongside each other). Already there are very necessary developments in the bibliographical control of databases, and the need for evaluation of content is an urgent one. (For some reason, users and librarians alike seem to have more implicit faith in the content of electronic media than in conventional print media – though of course in neither case is confidence necessarily justified.) Chapter 23 discusses the evaluation of databases in more detail. The general point to make at the outset is that the whole process of evaluating user needs and matching these to existing sources of information remains – whatever the format ultimately used to satisfy these needs.

3 Policy

No library can be effective without a *policy*, which sets out aims and objectives, identifies user groups and services, and indicates priorities amongst them. Since libraries are usually short of resources, prioritizing is an essential part of the process. The use of library budgets as a key instrument for prioritizing services is described in the next chapter.

Collection development is scarcely possible without a clear statement of library policy, though many librarians nevertheless try to manage without one. This chapter attempts to highlight some of the ways that policy considerations affect the provision of materials in academic and public libraries.

Academic libraries

Size of collection
An important policy matter which has been aired occasionally in recent years is the size of academic library collections, compared with the amount of use they receive. It is generally accepted in the 1990s that no academic library can be self-sufficient, and that academics must move around for materials (see Chapter 11 on 'weeding'). University libraries (particularly those in the United States, but also in the UK) tend to accumulate very large amounts of material indeed, as will be clear from reading the chapter on standards in this book. On the whole, these collections receive a low amount of use, particularly if the use of short loan collections is excluded from consideration. In fact, there is little doubt that a great many of the books and journals purchased by universities are not used at all. For instance, a study by Fussler and Simon[151] reported that over half the monographs accessioned by the University of Chicago Library during the years 1944 – 53 had

not been borrowed during the period 1953 – 8. A more recent research project by Kent[55] looked at monographs acquired by the University of Pittsburgh during the years 1969 – 75. Forty per cent (36,000 books) had not circulated, and any given book was reckoned to have a one in two chance of being borrowed. In another piece of research, Trueswell[307] formulated the theory that 80% of total circulation is normally propagated by 20% of a collection.

UK library studies are based on smaller collections, although the rate of use, where known, remains generally low. (Not surprisingly, many librarians are reluctant to put figures of this kind into print.) Use tends to be higher in UK polytechnics, where the emphasis is on teaching rather than research (see Castens[5]). A study in one polytechnic[292] found that 11% of the bookstock was in circulation, while in another[40] two samples taken from law and the humanities revealed that three issues per volume was the average use per annum, and that two-thirds of the items were loaned in a two-year period. It is perhaps a reflection of the overall picture in academic libraries that their rates of use were deemed to be quite good.

The development of massive and little used collections in universities has become a matter of custom – a practice scarcely requiring justification, unless taken to task. Articles by Gore[17] and by Cronin[14] are rare and eloquent examples of the critical approach. Heaney[5] puts a separate case for the defence. The most concerted attack upon the monolithic principle was the 1976 report of the UK University Grants Commission – *Capital provision for university libraries (the Atkinson report).*[28] Atkinson demanded for universities a 'self-renewing library of limited growth' (or 'steady state library'), which meant that beyond a certain point in size a library's acquisitions would be largely offset by the discarding of obsolete material. The self-renewing concept arose because the UGC was unwilling to provide the capital funding to extend university library buildings during the 1980s. They also reasoned that the costs of maintaining access to very large collections would erode funds available for new acquisitions.

Atkinson further recommended that universities should not hold large stocks in remote storage. As much as 85% of the materials should be on open access, and stock relegated to store should remain there for a trial period of five years before being returned

9

to the main library, or transferred to a permanent back-up collection such as the British Library. The report offered a norm for establishing a library's notional entitlement to space, achieved by multiplying the figure of 1.25 square metres by the planned number of full-time students.

At the time, Atkinson provoked a good deal of disgruntlement amongst university librarians, of which Steele's book[25] contained some representative examples. It was said that the report had advocated crude measures for dealing with a complex problem, and that not enough was known about the patterns of library use and the effects of browsing, literature obsolescence, or other factors, to put the future of university libraries at risk by wholesale withdrawals from stock at this stage of their development. The Atkinson definition of 'a reasonable size' was said to be too vague, and based upon existing levels of practice, rather than any desirable ideal. There were criticisms of the way that fundamentally different subjects, such as the humanities and the sciences, were to be treated in the same way. Librarians claimed that it was extremely difficult to predict a 'useful book', in research terms, and that those who retained only titles which were currently in demand would create serious problems for future researchers.

Fourteen years later, Atkinson might claim, at best, to have had a very modest effect. Some librarians do seem to be less concerned with the size of their collections, and more interested in access to them by users. There has been a renewal of interest and research into questions of obsolescence, and storage costs. A handful of universities have instituted weeding programmes.[304] But writing in 1987, Ford[5] could not identify any British university libraries conforming to the Atkinson mode. He observed that few libraries had developed a comprehensive approach to stock management, and that, on average, university libraries were acquiring eight times as many materials as they discarded. The questions which Atkinson posed have yet to be addressed.

Level

To the extent that academic libraries serve a captive and easily defined audience, their collection development is more straightforward than, say, in the public library sphere. All the same there are considerable variations in the needs of different user groups, both by subject and by level. In the matter of level, these needs range from the relatively simple requirements of undergraduate students, through to the wide and unpredictable needs of researchers and faculty. Decisions on priorities between these groups can generate some heat, particularly if students come to believe that their needs are taking second place to those of numerically smaller groups of faculty and researchers. The controversy is more pronounced in university libraries than in the UK polytechnics, where the emphasis is upon teaching rather than research, and where there are few special collections of the kind to be found in universities.

Most universities differentiate undergraduate provision quite sharply by housing the best-used textbooks in short loan collections, where decisions upon duplication are based upon careful monitoring of loan statistics (see pp.34 – 5). It would be rare to come across policy statements which are explicit about the level of provision accorded to undergraduates *vis-à-vis* other groups, but some universities develop rule of thumb guidelines – for instance, a maximum number of copies for undergraduate texts, or (commonly) a rule restricting research material to single copies.

Periodicals remain by far the most important research tool for academics, both for current awareness scanning and for chasing up citations to individual articles. In recent years most academic libraries have been forced to cut back on periodical provision, to prevent serials from running away with unreasonable proportions of their budgets for materials (see pp.135 – 8). Even so, periodicals often take some 45% of the total funding for materials.

Subject

In addition to settling priorities between levels of provision, university librarians must also prioritize between subjects. The resourcing of higher education in the UK is increasingly based upon allocations for fixed student number targets for different subjects, with a set unit of resource allocated per student. But the allocation of library resources between subjects does not necessarily follow a logical or easily summarized method. Much depends upon past practice and university politics. Use is not necessarily a major factor, and Peasgood's article[66] describing changes in allocations between faculties according to past use probably reflects the exception rather than the rule. Higham's book[114] describes how decisions are made in practice, including

11

the way that inter-faculty disputes can be resolved in library committees.

A university's research resources are an important factor in funding. Tucker's article[26] on developing research collections in the new universities is one of those rare pieces which gives the feel of this subject. He makes the point that research collection developments often owe a good deal to chance, in addition to the institution's stated priorities. He observes that universities do not usually have research policies as such, and that the librarian therefore receives little guidance on new directions for collection development. Special collections purchased from private or public sources may form the bulk of a university's holdings of research materials, and the acquisition of one special collection may – if it is subsequently well maintained – lead to the offer of further collections in the same field. In another informative paper, Heaney[5] argues that special collection development policies should be committed to paper. Priorities should be assessed, and while some special collections may be left as they are, others should be developed assiduously.

Public libraries

Types of service
The functions of academic and special libraries appear positively clear-cut when compared with those of their counterparts in the public library field. Uncertainty over objectives has bedevilled public libraries for many years. The various official statements are unhelpful in practice. The British Public Libraries Act of 1964, for instance, stipulates[294] 'by the keeping of adequate stocks, by arrangements with other library authorities, and by any other appropriate means, that facilities are available for the borrowing of, or reference to, books . . . and other materials sufficient in number, range, and quality to meet the general requirements and any special requirements both of adults and children'. UNESCO's *Public library manifesto*[27] gives a similarly broad definition of public library objectives. The Public Library Research Group definition of public library aims reads[18] 'To contribute to sustaining the quality of life in all aspects – educational, economic, industrial, scientific and cultural . . .', and is followed by a sub-statement on adult lending services 'To satisfy the educational, informational

12

and recreational needs of the community ...'.

Anyone who has been associated with the realities of public library provision will know that these Olympian objectives are unachievable, particularly at present. As resources become increasingly scarce, choices have to be made and priorities set. Some authorities have developed explicit policies which establish priorities amongst the various types of service referred to above. Others have muddled through without a policy, although in that situation choices are still forced willy-nilly upon those who select materials. Before we look at these choices, the various types of service warrant an attempt at definition.

The phrase *educational reading* is often used in the sense of textbooks for formal education programmes. This is not a major precoccupation of public libraries, although in Britain, for instance, authorities are expected to provide back-up texts for Open University courses. In terms of self-education or self-development (or whatever term is used), the provision of educational material has always been very much part of the public library's brief. Many of the appropriate works are likely to be for users who require a general introduction to a subject – even though, in some cases, the same user's formal education may be highly advanced in another field. Jones noted in a useful survey of 12 public library authorities[269] that 20% – 35% of the material on adult non-fiction shelves was 'popular', 33% – 40% elementary, 25% – 30% 'standard', and only 10% – 15% advanced.

The *information* function of public libraries probably needs little definition. To a considerable extent it shades into the self-education function, especially if the latter is broadened to include practical matters (do-it-yourself, cookery, sport, etc.).

Recreational reading can be defined as a pastime by which the reader fills in time pleasantly. In the Western world (though not often in developing countries) many public library users read recreationally at one time or another, and large numbers of people read in this way almost exclusively. Over half the issues of British public libraries can be ascribed to recreational reading, although – as will be seen – public libraries are rarely arranged to suit the recreational approach.

The ungainly term *cultural reading* alludes to a function which is notoriously difficult to define. Benge[242] refers to reading which is

13

useless in any direct sense, but always important in any society. It involves the disinterested pursuit of truth, beauty or goodness, even though it is always mixed up with other motivations such as the search for social importance (knowledge is power), or for status and acceptance, or for the comforts of a dream world, or for the individual self-realisation which involves the establishment of a personal identity.

It may loosely be judged to refer to at least some of the works of literature, art, philosophy, history and biography.

It is suggested above that no public library can satisfy demand for all these types of material – least of all at a time of diminishing resources. Choices have to be made, whether by management or by those who actually select material. An important example of this is the balance that must be struck between the information/ education and the recreational/cultural functions. Alexander Wilson[290] has called the latter the 'theatre of recorded entertainment'. It is, he says, 'the evangelising role, the exciting role, the impresario role, the recreational role . . .'. He argues that this service is much more appropriately organized at local level, where demand for the theatre of books can be stimulated, whilst the information function operates essentially at national level, in response to demand. 'I cannot understand', Wilson says,

> Why we have gone so long using our branch network as though it were doing the information job. These libraries, large and small, are organised on the assumption that people come to them as a knowledge materials distribution centre, knowing what they want. We respond – ping/pong. That is not what most people come for at all. A great majority of them are looking for the theatre of books, and it is not there.

Chapters 20 and 21 of this book give detailed attention to 'fiction' – overwhelmingly the main preoccupation of public library users – and to the related fields of biography and travel writing.

Types of user
The main controversy in British public libraries over the past decade has concerned choices between different types of user. Recent books by McKee[23] and Usherwood[29] reflect typical preoccupations. Local government services, afflicted by heavy cut-

backs, have also been characterized by increasing politicization.

Some authorities have taken direct political action (see below). Others have moved away from responsive services for traditional public library targets to concentrate their resources on outreach services to the disadvantaged sections of communities – specialized information facilities, collections for minority user groups, and so on. In effect, decisions of this kind are also, if indirectly, political.

These are difficult waters for the professional. Library collections have to be developed, whatever the deeper political or sociological undercurrents. There seem to be at least four overlapping requirements for librarians to take into account. Firstly, the need to take the use of collections into full consideration. Secondly, the need to make decisions about priorities. Thirdly, the need to avoid censorship. Fourthly, the need for collections to reflect the full range of materials available within the priority areas chosen. These requirements are discussed below.

The need for user studies has been widely discussed in the past decade, and Chapter 4 of this book looks at the very considerable recent literature on the subject. Studies of use, and of potential use, are an essential prerequisite for the sort of value judgements (see below) which must be made about book provision. In Britain a key document – the Hillingdon report[306] – examined the effectiveness of public library attempts to satisfy user needs, and concluded that most public library services were 'supplier-oriented'. This meant, Hillingdon concluded, that 'needs have a predetermined boundary deriving from the people who are supplying the library service and reflecting their own cultural and educational goals. In this situation a distinction is almost always made between significant needs and by implication unimportant wants or desires.'

These are valid points, but there should be some sympathy for practising librarians who have to develop policy in difficult circumstances. Faced with a wide range of demands and severe shortages of funding, they must make decisions about priorities, and in the last analysis the creation of a scheme of priorities for provision – though based upon a complex pattern of evidence about user requirements – must in part be the result of the librarian's own judgement. There are no simplistic formulae for judging the 'correct' proportions for the allocation of funding or for resolving contradictions inherent in the situation. Benge comments, in a valuable section from his *Bibliography and the provision of books*[241] that

> those who state simply that a public library exists to provide people with what they want forget that the library service itself is one of the agencies which determine what they want. All agencies of mass culture, i.e. the press, the radio, the television and the cinema, stand in this dialectical relation to the individual and must in the last resort concern themselves with value judgements.

Unfortunately, in this heated debating chamber we also find – uninvited and unwelcome – the heavily masked delegate for 'censorship'. It is essential to distinguish between, on the one hand, attaching priorities to different types of service or service to particular user groups, and on the other ensuring that certain types of material, reflecting certain views, are excluded from libraries altogether. A recent article on this theme[24] brought both censors and defenders of free expression out of the woodwork and into the correspondence columns of the *Library Association record*. A disturbing number of librarians now appear to believe that their jobs may legitimately be used to proselytize, for political and other beliefs, and to be unaware that these are highly damaging views for librarians to hold. The euphemism 'positive selection policies' has been devised to soften censorship's image. Bob Usherwood's comment[29] that there is 'a degree of tension' between 'positive selection policy' and 'commitment to intellectual freedom' adopts a distinctly uncomfortable posture on the fence. McClellan provided the definitive judgement many years ago,[283] and it is one which is only partially vitiated by recent developments in local government. 'The public library is the only channel of communication of ideas and feelings which is not controlled either by powerful minority interests or by monopolies. The public library uniquely affords the expression of all minority views, gives all of them the opportunity of acceptance, or of withering away. Its existence in the form we know is a guarantee of intellectual and political freedom.'

Perhaps the last word might go to L. R. McColvin, whose views on the relationship between book provision and demand make interesting reading 35 years after they were written. McColvin's early work *Theory of book selection for public libraries*,[21] which postulated demand as the principal criterion for provision, is repudiated in an article he published some 30 years later. In 'Some administrative aspects of book provision'[22] McColvin urges the provision of a comprehensive *coverage* of stock in public libraries, in which librarians purchase everything that is 'worthwhile', reject (bad books) rather than select, and omit to buy only material which readers can obtain more easily from other sources. This does not tackle head on the various problems of priority raised above, but the principle of minimum coverage seems a very good starting point for a public librarian, allowing value judgements to concern themselves with the *degree* of provision attempted within the overall coverage. In effect, a public library which attempts basic coverage of material for minority as well as majority interests is introducing a controlled bias in favour of the minority. This is discussed in more detail in Chapter 10 on logistics.

Books or other materials
One other matter of priority perhaps warrants discussion. British public libraries have in the past 10 years diversified very considerably by providing their public with access to a variety of non-book materials. Music records and cassettes (and now compact discs), videos, computer software and other materials are all discussed in the following pages. For the most part these diversifications have been well received by their users. One influential dissenting voice has talked of priorities being established in this area too. The Minister for Arts, Richard Luce, speaking at the Library Association Members' Day in 1987, remarked, 'We must ensure that we do not lose sight of our main objective. I will tell you plainly that so far as I am concerned that objective is the promotion of books ....'

Policy statements
The range of available options – particularly in public libraries – means that every library system needs a book provision policy, in which the priorities for provision are laid down. This is particularly important when funding is limited and hard choices have therefore to be made. To be of real use the policy statement should be specific about priorities and other matters. Broad statements of intent ('the library takes account of varying needs

17

... anticipates future requirements and current demands ...'
etc.) are of little practical use – although many policy statements
consist almost entirely of generalizations along these lines.

As well as being a means of communication for staff, to ensure
consistency of approach, a selection policy may serve other
functions. It can be a planning tool for the library management,
a statement of purpose for the board or governing body, and a
source of information for library users – though on the last point
some libraries may find it politic not to make known priorities
so openly to their public.

Examples of policy statements have been published in a book
edited by Futas.[16] A survey by Apted[12] suggested that perhaps
a quarter to a third of university libraries have selection policy
statements of some kind. The situation appears to be similar in
UK public libraries, where a survey by Capital Planning
Information[13] found that one-third of 32 library authorities
surveyed had some form of selection policy.

The last-named survey listed the kind of information that was
contained in selection policies. This included: the relationship of
the material selected to the libraries' objectives; guidance on levels
of provision in different sizes of library; criteria for selection;
definition of community groups to be served; policy on censorship;
comments on various types of material – e.g. paperbacks,
audiovisual materials; donations policy; relationships with the book
trade; statements of responsibility for selection; demographic
information about the area. The full list makes something of a
hodgepodge, and it is probably more sensible to take the course
adopted by some authorities, and separate 'policy' from 'methods'.

There is a real difficulty about producing genuinely useful policy
documents, since they need to define priorities and services in
a way that is meaningful to both policy makers and policy
executors. Whilst most user groups can be identified with relative
ease, the various types of material or service often resist clear
definition. One may easily state, for instance, that no more than
25% of fiction funds will be spent on light fiction, but the statement
is unhelpful unless all parties involved will readily recognize an
item of light fiction when they see one. The level of material is
also hard to pin down with workable definitions. The effectiveness
of policy guidelines therefore depends upon good general
communications between policy makers and other staff, as well

18

as clear and unambiguous statements in the guidelines themselves.

Given both these features, written policies are still likely to remain pious statements of intent unless supported by financial mechanisms. It is essential that specific resources are allocated to stated priorities, and that expenditure is subsequently monitored to ensure that funds are properly spent. The subject is covered in detail in the following chapter.

4 Budgeting

Under the headings of 'academic' and 'public' libraries, this chapter examines two subjects. Firstly, how is the budget figure for library materials achieved? Secondly, how is that figure divided up, or allocated – that is, how is the library's policy translated into financial terms?

Public libraries

Budgets

Public library budgets, including bookfunds, derive from the budgeting procedures carried out within local authorities. For various reasons the size of a public library's bookfund is more often the result of circumstances and local politics than of reasoned calculation. Until recent years the aim of the librarian, more often than not, was to achieve as large an increase on his previous year's bookfund as his finance committee would tolerate. In the economic climate of the 1980s and 1990s ambitions tend to be more modest, and most librarians would now be happy to achieve a figure which is equal to the previous year, with an increase to cover risen costs.

Records of public library authority budgets – estimates and actuals – are issued annually by the Chartered Institute of Public Finance and Accountancy.[256] The 1988/89 'actuals' show that on average public library authorities in that year spent 50% of their budgets on staffing, 16% on books, and 10% on premises (with the other 12% on debt charges and central establishment costs). In public libraries, 'bookfund' does largely mean expenditure on books, with a relatively small commitment to periodicals and other materials.

There is no 'correct' way for a librarian to calculate the desirable size of his bookfund, but taking into account published standards plus a variety of factors which affect the use and condition of his stock he can devise a semi-scientific approach. McClellan's work furnishes basic formulae for calculations of this kind.[287] Such formulae are complex and not easily resolved since the relevant factors cannot all be readily equated, and in any case are not all quantifiable. Briefly, these factors are: the total population of the area and the number of registered library members; trends in book publishing – i.e. the number of new books published per annum, broken down by subjects; the length of life of stock on the open shelves (depreciation rate); the risen costs of books and binding on the previous year's fund; and the range and condition of the existing stock.

Major changes of policy or new developments in an authority may also affect funding for materials – as, for instance, at the opening of a new service point. However, stock purchased for growth or expansion is normally regarded as capital expenditure and is therefore not considered for the purposes of recurrent funding.

A procedure adopted by some authorities to estimate recurrent expenditure is to assume that user needs and the number of new titles required are fairly constant and to allow simply for an increase in the price of materials. Ideally the calculations for increased prices should be broken down into different categories of material and related to the number of volumes purchased by the library in each of these categories. Most public libraries are content with very broad categories (non-fiction, fiction, children's books). Six-monthly lists of average book prices, broken down by subject field, are published in the *Bookseller* and republished in the *Library Association record*. Some library authorities work out their own average book prices based on accessions to stock, so that the figures relate more closely to their actual needs. Estimates extrapolated from past trends in this way should be checked by monitoring the price actually paid for books, and subsequently adjusting where necessary.[293]

'Depreciation rate' is a term sometimes used to describe the rate of physical decline of existing stock to a point where it is so decrepit as to be no longer usable. Information about depreciation rates must be derived from a number of different sources. McClellan gives as a crude yardstick a book life of 60 issues for fiction and children's books and 75 issues for non-fiction.[286] Houghton suggests 80 – 100 issues over 5 – 7 years for hardbacks and 30 – 40 issues for paperbacks.[267] A Hertfordshire survey reports,[303] from an analysis of withdrawals, an average of nine years for the life of a hardback. An Australian survey[295] gives eight years. (Another way of interpreting, for instance, this last figure, is to deduce an annual replacement figure of 12.5% of total existing stock.) These figures vary, as they are bound to do, with differences in types of books stocked, binding policies, local circumstances, and – especially – the size of local bookfunds and therefore the minimum physical standard of stock that can be fixed pragmatically by each authority. Authorities are therefore best advised to conduct their own experiments to reach a realistic depreciation figure.

The rate of 'obsolescence' (i.e. decline in use through age) is a much more complex phenomenon, and is also difficult to quantify in a generalized way. Figures must be constructed for particular subjects in a particular situation (see p.89).

The number of new books being published is relevant to funding needs. Normally, increases or reductions in publishing output tend to be undramatic, but in the 1980s the numbers of new titles published annually have gone up very substantially indeed – increases not on the whole matched by additions to library bookfunds.

The range and quality of the existing stock is also an important factor. A period of under-provision over a number of years is likely to be reflected on the shelves in subject gaps or in the poor physical condition of stock. However, a quantification of this factor in numbers of volumes or in cost is extremely difficult to achieve. Only where under-provision has resulted in really serious deficiencies is it likely that a librarian can argue successfully for extra funding to put the balance right. In fact few library authorities make a serious attempt at tackling problems of stock logistics, so that this factor is rarely quantified, except in a very general sense.

For that matter the whole process of reaching an annual bookfund figure is usually somewhat arbitrary, and the foregoing comments may be taken more as background than as an analysis of the way chief librarians go about reaching a total. In practice, national or local restrictions (or lack of restrictions) on public spending are far more likely to influence the eventual figure reached than are formulae involving use and depreciation of stock, and the librarian may find that the most useful lever for increasing his estimates before his finance committee is his comparative position – in relation to comparable systems – in the league table of local authority bookfunds.

Allocation

Just as the size of the bookfund determines the overall standard of stock provision that can be achieved, its allocation within the authority should determine the standard of provision for particular categories of stock.

Effective allocation of funds, and subsequent monitoring of expenditure, is the basis for ensuring that library policy (as discussed in the previous chapter) is translated into provision. The American Library Association's *Guidelines for the allocation of library materials budgets*[31] gives a useful discussion of the principles of allocation without attempting any practical recommendations. In Britain, the lack of any national guidelines for allocation, and the reluctance of librarians to air the subject in the professional press, have contributed towards a situation where, in many public library authorities, there is a distinct credibility gap between policy and achievement.

The degree of central control exercised over provision in British public library authorities varies considerably. The major change of emphasis in the past 25 years has been the breakdown of the bookfund into headings representing functional or user criteria rather than into geographical headings. Few library authorities now give allocations to individual service points, since the benefits of gearing stock provision to a larger geographical area are widely recognized. In many of the county libraries, however, financial control is largely, or almost entirely, delegated to the zones or areas. On occasion, zones will be requested to submit notional breakdowns on their expenditure for the forthcoming year, but such submissions are often no more than the haziest guides to real expenditure. In such circumstances a central control of expenditure, and therefore of policy, is not possible.

Where allocations are made to individual service points, a number of factors may be taken into account in deciding the division of funds. One of these is the size of existing stocks, considered together with various logistic factors discussed in Chapter 10. (Moore's article[95] gives a useful discussion of these.) The dependence here upon *existing* stock sizes is an obvious disadvantage, and can be counterbalanced to some extent by allocating on the basis of use – though even this will in part at least reflect existing conditions. Whatever the basis of allocation, small service points will need an additional weighting if they are to maintain a reasonable range of materials.

Nearly all authorities – even the most decentralized – reserve some money under central control to purchase material which the zones do not want, or cannot afford, or simply as a fund to cover emergencies. This allocation is variously known as the contingency fund or the reserve (or in at least one authority as 'the slosh'). Such an allocation commonly absorbs about 10% – 20% of the bookfund.

As suggested above, rather more control over policy can be maintained if allocation is by criteria other than geographical ones, and many authorities allocate at least part of their bookfunds on the basis of function, user groups, or formats of material. Amongst criteria commonly used are:

Function The need for clarification of function in public libraries has already been discussed in Chapter 3. Guidelines may relate generically to a function (e.g. recreational reading, adult literacy materials, textbooks collections, reference material, foreign language books) or to more specific categories of books within the function (e.g. within recreational reading, to romances or popular biographies). The priority to be accorded to light fiction needs particular attention.

User groups Children's provision is almost invariably separated, with allocations varying from 12% – 20% of the total. Other groups commonly separated are hospitals, housebound readers, and prisons.

Subject Public libraries tend to budget by subject only if the staff is organized into subject specialist groups. However, certain subject areas may be singled out for special treatment in any authority, either for local reasons (e.g. subject fields relating to local industries) or simply from a sense of commitment to the public library's responsibilities in certain areas (e.g. current affairs, the arts). Most public libraries allocate separately for fiction and for music. Certain service points may be designated as repositories for subject collections. Alternatively, some subjects may be best served by the building up of circulating subject collections, for which special allocation would generally be made.

Format Many public libraries now spend large sums on paperbacks, and budget for them separately. Most also budget separately for audiovisual materials, playsets and microforms.

Level Most public library authorities place a strong emphasis on introductory materials and standard works, rather than on advanced material. However, this emphasis is rarely quantified in the budget.

In addition to the above, annuals are normally covered by standing orders, which eliminate repetitive clerical work. Some public libraries (and more frequently, university libraries) also place standing orders for all the works in a series. The content of standing order lists should be regularly reviewed, especially when their percentage of the total expenditure begins to rise. Material which is variable in approach or content (as in some series) should not be acquired through standing order.

An allocation is usually set aside to cover the purchase of readers' requests (for older material).

Binding costs are normally estimated separately.

This brief résumé of methods of allocation omits an important area which is rarely controlled through financial allocation, yet which certainly needs to be subjected to some form of central control. This is the relative expenditure on *stock revision* as opposed to selection from 'new' books. The matter is discussed in detail in Chapter 9, where it is suggested that the quality of stock on the shelves can only be maintained through extensive stock revision, and that most public library authorities would at present benefit from allocating at least 40% of their bookfunds to stock revision.

Although monitored allocations of the kind suggested above are the only way to ensure that library policy is translated into practice, it would be unrealistic to believe that all authorities manage their budgets in this way. The recent survey *Trends in public library selection policies*[13] shows that about 20% of public libraries do not even allocate to categories such as adult fiction, or children's books, and very few record stock revision separately.

Budgets

Fifty-five per cent of university funding in Britain comes from public money. The major part is a recurrent grant paid by the government to the Universities Funding Council, which allocates funds to individual universities. Funding for polytechnics and colleges of higher education (both now independent of local authorities) comes from central government via the Polytechnics and Colleges Funding Council. In addition, universities and polytechnics commonly derive substantial funding from endowments, or from grants and gifts from foundations and benefactors. And they increasingly make revenue from research and consultancy services for commercial firms.

The way that university library budgets are calculated is changing, and there is no reliable overview of current practice. More often than not, university library budgets relate to materials and running costs, but not to staffing, which is handled centrally. Graham (whose chapter on budgeting and allocating[33] is essential reading) reports a survey of 23 university libraries he carried out in 1985, in which 14 of the library grants covered only non-staffing costs (books, periodicals, binding and operational money), whilst the other nine included staffing, though usually with severe limitations on virement between staffing and other sub-heads. Graham also reported that 12 of the 23 librarians had provided some form of budget estimates, though most of these had related largely to maintaining the existing value of materials funds by reporting on risen costs, from information such as the twice-yearly *Average prices of British academic books*[240] and Blackwells's information on periodical prices,[244] together with other factors discussed in the section on public library budgeting above.

Fletcher[32] reported a similar picture on polytechnic funding. For instance, Coventry Polytechnic library's budget again excluded staffing, and was divided into five headings: 1. equipment, 2. repairs and maintenance, 3. subscriptions (to memberships of organizations), 4. travel and subsistence and 5. materials.

The inter-library comparison of 14 university libraries carried out by the Centre for Interfirm Comparison in 1979/80[255] showed how staff costs are predominating over the budgets for materials. The breakdown of expenditure for the libraries concerned showed (all median percentages): books 19%; serials 15%; staff 56%; binding 5%; sundries 6%. (These figures excluded building maintenance.)

Graham commented that in practice budgeting was usually a matter of upgrading funding based on historical foundations rather than calculating what was required for the services that were needed, and he referred to university funding being 'budget-led' rather than 'product-led'. But the overall basis of academic library funding is changing significantly. The trend is towards a steady reduction in government funding, together with a policy of requiring universities and polytechnics to bid for funds in new ways. Funding is increasingly allocated on the basis of taught student numbers and/or research students numbers (this applies to library funding too.) Formulas of this kind can only be the starting point in a process which always demands a sophisticated approach. The point is that financial management in the 1990s requires librarians (and all other service managers) to provide a justification for funding bids, rather than to expect money to be granted as of right.

Allocations

Resource allocation – between types of material and/or between subjects (or departments) – is a function of library policy, and has a profound effect upon collection development. Allocation decisions are made by the Librarian, or by the Librarian in conjunction with the library committee (largely comprised of academics), or by the library committee alone.

It is common for funding to be split between books and periodicals, since these two types of material are acquired in different ways, and in this case book funding is almost always further subdivided by subject. But some libraries subdivide initially by subject, allowing the department to sort out relative expenditure on books and periodicals. Both systems can be made to work.

The subject of *formulas* for allocations is a controversial one, discussed by Graham and by Budd.[252] Some 40% – 50% of UK academic libraries appear to use these devices in one way or another. Amongst the variables suggested for arriving at formulas are: volume of publishing and costs of materials; statistics of circulation and other types of use; student and/or staff numbers; research output; number of courses. Formulas have two particular advantages. They are (one hopes) *seen* to be fair, and are thus politically acceptable. And they are responsive to change, and so forestall the inflexibility of 'historical' allocations. There are also disadvantages. The figures used are not always reliable indicators. It is difficult to combine them in a valid mathematical relationship. And experience suggests that to rely upon figures alone, excluding critical judgement, will distort the allocation process or lead to an impractical approach being adopted. For instance past spending behaviour is always likely to be a factor in practice, with departments which have been reliable spenders more likely to be given funds than those who have been allocated money but not spent it. Higham's book[114] contains an informative section upon the politics of dividing up a bookfund, and on the necessary procedures for monitoring and managing expenditure to ensure that all funds are committed, and that commitment follows an even pace throughout the year.

Further comments on attaching priorities to different subjects and to different levels of material are to be found in Chapter 3.

5 *Users*

Book provision is invariably concerned with service to a specified clientele – e.g. the members of an association, the staff and students of an academic institution, or (in a public library) the inhabitants of a geographical area. The policy considerations underlying provision are largely determined by the nature of the parent institution, or in the case of public libraries by national legislation. However, these underlying guidelines, whilst helpful in a general way, do not provide enough specific information to guide book provision in any detail. In practice demand invariably outstrips supply, obliging librarians to make decisions upon priorities. The *needs of the library's users* must provide the basis for such decisions, and librarians must make every effort to see that the full extent of these needs is known, in all their range and variety. This is the single most important factor in effective book provision.

For a variety of reasons, connected with the nature of the literature and the nature of users, a knowledge of user needs is by no means an easy thing to achieve. Until relatively recently little was known, but the position has been improved by a large number of studies in the past 25 years. This chapter briefly surveys the nature of user needs and the factors which bear upon use, and then attempts to summarize the methods by which use can be studied and analysed.

In the UK two small research centres have been helpful in focusing progress on user studies, and in developing reliable methods. The Centre for Research on User Studies functioned from 1975 to 1985, from the University of Sheffield. Its work has recently been summarized in an article by Roberts and Wilson.[67] The Library Management Research Unit was established in Cambridge University to investigate problems in the organization of university libraries and the use made of their services by readers. The unit moved to Loughborough University in 1976, where its title was subsequently changed to the Centre for Library and Information Management (CLAIM), and where its new objectives are to improve the effectiveness of service to users.

The British National Bibliography Research Fund, established in 1975, includes amongst its aims the promotion of research into the use of books and into reading habits, and has achieved an impact beyond its modest resources – as a glance at the bibliography of this book will show. The research sponsored by the fund has been usefully summarized in an article by Greenwood.[47]

In a voluminous literature on the measurement of library use, two general surveys are essential reading. Geoffrey Ford's *Review of methods employed in determining the use of library stock*,[45] published in 1990, reviews data collection methods and the interpretation of findings, and factors associated with book use, referring to 135 surveys in his bibliography. Lancaster's *If you want to evaluate your library ...*[57] gives a concise survey of use evaluation methods.

From the welter of information available, perhaps the most significant point to emerge from user studies is that few, if any, of their findings lend themselves to general applicability. Vickery has written: 'Most of the conclusions that can be drawn from studies of people and information are either very general or specific to particular social groups, or even particular organisations.' The message seems to be that librarians must determine the most accurate methods for studying use in their own libraries, and carry out their own research.

Finally, by way of introduction, Ranganathan's laws of librarianship remain valid to the study of library use: books are for use; for every reader his book; for every book its reader; save the time of the user.

The nature of user needs

A rare approach to library use from the *reader's* point of view is Frank Hatt's *The reading process*,[50] of which the first two chapters are essential reading. Hatt emphasizes the gap between the approach of librarians, working from a firm base of known documents and systems, and that of users, trying to locate and match to their own (often ill-defined) requirements documents not yet known to exist.

The Hillingdon report on public library effectiveness[73] distinguished between users' expressed needs, and their unexpressed or unactivated needs. Under the first definition, users were deemed to be visiting a library with the particular intention of searching for a document or for information. Explicit indicators of expressed need are reservations and spoken enquiries (sometimes referred to collectively as 'demand'), and also logistic studies (see Chapter 10) and circulation statistics.

Hillingdon's thesis was that 'unexpressed needs', though felt, had not been seen in terms of a library solution, whilst in the case of 'unactivated need' the library stimulated demand for needs which had not even been felt. In recent years many British public libraries have increased the proportion of their resources committed to satisfying unexpressed need, by taking staff away from the library base to work in institutions in the community, and by changing the nature of collections to appeal to groups who had not previously seen public libraries as providing a service useful to them.

Use and benefit

Although a considerable amount of generalized research on use has been carried out, many librarians still know relatively little about what their users want. They may not have information about users' success (or lack of it) in searching for particular books, or for books on particular subjects, or the extent to which users locate substitutes for their original choices, or the extent to which users browse or take up materials on impulse, or the manner in which impulse choices are taken up. Even less is known about the usefulness of books which *are* located and borrowed, and it is quite likely that many of the titles thought to have answered a subject enquiry are not in fact found by the reader to be very useful at all. Yet, as Lancaster observes[272] 'Librarians do not exist merely to acquire books or to maximise the work load at the circulation desk: presumably libraries are in some way concerned with certain uses of books and with certain desired outcomes of the reading process.'

This question of the *benefit* to be achieved from library activities has generated a good deal of literature, none of it very conclusive. Orr's article[64] provides a good summary of the problems faced in trying to establish any form of benefit. On the positive side, market penetration may be said to represent some sort of indicator. For instance, academic libraries, with captive audiences, generally attract 75% – 90% of their institutions' complement of students and staff to borrow books. Public libraries (without a captive audience) average a membership of 30% of the population. Membership *renewal* rate is a classic indicator of success – particularly so if fees are charged.

On the specific matter of benefit related to use, Ford writes[261]

> . . . it has been suggested that the value of an activity may be related to the time expended by the user. This certainly seems to be true if we consider that at the time the activity (such as using a book) takes place, the person concerned is certainly doing it in preference to doing anything else. So measures of document exposure may be the only direct measures of the benefits of book use which are relatively easy to collect and to compute.

If this is accepted, in-house studies of use and surveys soliciting user opinions are amongst the most significant use measures.

Features bearing upon use

Ford's book gives an invaluable summary of 'factors associated with book use'. So many different factors may be relevant that no generalized conclusions can be reached, and the best that librarians can do is to ensure that as far as possible conditions for use in their own libraries are adapted to meet what research has revealed as ideal conditions.

Use is certainly affected by some characteristics relating to the user – notably the fact that users from different disciplines have different information requirements, and use the literature in different ways. Some references, from a considerable list, are given in the bibliography to this chapter.[43, 52, 70, 71, 62]

Another substantial literature, recently surveyed by Craghill,[44] relates to public library use. Here users tend to come from a wide variety of backgrounds, and press for an equally wide range of requirements. Luckham's survey[60] was one of the largest and best known. A further set of influences relate to the materials themselves. Publication date is a factor, though it must be interpreted with care (see p.89 on obsolescence). Language is also significant (see pp.140 – 4). Physical format can affect use – small print, for instance, or the fact that oversized books and pamphlets are located separately and therefore are more difficult to find.

A whole range of accessibility factors also bear upon use of library materials. The location of the library in relation to users is important, but so too is the location of stock within the library. For instance, books are used more frequently if placed on shelves which are of convenient height (rather than too high or too low), and if put on special display outside the main sequence (see p.155).

Finally, on the subject of accessibility, stock is used more frequently if kept on open rather than closed access, because of the importance to users of *browsing* as a method of locating material (see Goodall's book for a summary of recent literature on the beguiling topic of browsing[46]). Ford estimates that in academic libraries as much as one-third of all items used are found by discovery at the shelf, and in public libraries about half the books borrowed are located in this way. Surveys of in-house library use are described below.

Aspects of user studies

Some of the most common aspects of use study are examined below – viz. circulation, in-house use, and document availability. An important point is that nearly all the methods which measure use must by definition relate to use of libraries' existing collections, and thus reflect their existing limitations. Building a stock exclusively upon the results of this kind of study is bound to lead eventually to some distortion between requirements and provision. For this reason, the concept of basic coverage of subjects and levels is urged (see pp.16 – 17).

Circulation

The most widely-known and applied measures of library use relate to circulation. They have some obvious disadvantages. For instance, a book issued is not necessarily a book read, and a book read has not (as discussed above) necessarily given its reader what he or she wanted. But despite their limitations, circulation measures can provide librarians with a good deal of valuable information for the assessment of stock and user needs, and the promoters of automated circulation systems have been quick to point out the facilities such systems offer for a closer analysis of detail.

Such systems may be used for a variety of purposes. A daily, monthly, annual etc. count of issues within particular subject areas can provide guidance to the popularity (or otherwise) of sections of the stock, particularly if the breakdown of subjects is sufficiently detailed. A subject breakdown of books on loan at any one time, compared with books in those same subject areas remaining on the shelves, gives a different perspective. The whole matter of quantitative information about stock – particularly when used to diagnose stock revision requirements – is explored in more detail in Chapter 10 of this book on 'logistics'.

Another method is to take a sample of titles or subject areas and follow the progress of the sample over a number of years. One of the largest surveys of this kind was the University of Pittsburgh study.[55] Peasgood, in a more recent exercise,[66] described how studies of subject use in an academic library revealed considerable variations, and led to changes in allocations policy. He noted however that few computer-based circulation systems include as standard features the ability to cumulate data over a period of years, or to analyse the data as required, so that much in-house development of existing systems was necessary.

Another range of measures based upon circulation data are designed to predict future use from past use. These are mainly used for weeding stock, and are described in Chapter 11.

Many automated systems permit libraries to track the circulation records of individual volumes, particularly in academic libraries where, if use rises above a certain threshold, the volume may be transferred from the main stock sequence to the short loans collection. And of course most issue systems lead to the books themselves carrying a record of past loans on their date labels. This humble record – the date stamp – should not be undervalued, since a loan history on the book may be correlated during the weeding process with other factors (physical condition, the content of other shelf stock) in a way that cannot be achieved through automated systems.

The most intensively automated sections of any library are probably the short loan collections of universities, where books in high demand are separately shelved and issued for varying brief periods of a few days down to a few hours on one day. Buckland's early paper on this subject[41] pointed out that the Librarian's capacity to determine official loan periods gives him 'a powerful and precise device for influencing the availability of books in his library'. He concluded: 'the cardinal rule of library stock control is that both the loan period and the duplication policy should be related to the level of demand for the title and to each other.' Short loans collections are often responsible for half of the total circulation of an academic library, and automated circulation analysis permits a high degree of accuracy in decisions on the quantities and loan status of titles retained there.

Overton[65] reviewed the kinds of management information available from 32 British academic libraries with automated circulation systems. She found that of the 16 libraries which retained archive files of statistics, the following principal uses were recorded: monitoring book use for duplication of titles (10 libraries); fund allocation (5); monitoring book use for change of loan status of books (5); and for relegation purposes (5); examination of interdisciplinary use of stock (3); monitoring loans for possible changes in loan regulations (2).

Overton describes three different types of information obtained from automated systems – statistical, operational and analytical. *Statistical* information, principally loan counts, is analysed by category of borrowers and by department (to show the characteristics of active readership) and by subject (for purposes of fund allocation). The total number of loaned items is also matched against total loanable stock, to show the proportion of live stock. *Operational* records are described as giving day-to-day information such as lists of books issued to each user or listings giving the whereabouts of books not on the shelves. These are used, for instance, to determine whether the same items keep cropping up and require duplication or allocation to short loan collections, and also to identify missing titles and replace them. *Analytical* records are described as a cumulation of statistical and operational, plus information from other files. Examples given are: a league table of the use of each title in the main library and the short loans collection, to determine titles that should be duplicated or marked for reference use; a record of items never used, for relegation purposes; records of the use of books by subject, including interdisciplinary use, for purposes of fund allocation; and analysis of the use of books by date of publication, to determine obsolescence parameters.

In-house use

Circulation statistics considerably under-represent use of library stock, because they take no account of in-house use – that is, use of material inside the library rather than outside.

Research leaves no doubt that a considerable amount of in-house use takes place. For instance the University of Pittsburgh study found that in-house use largely correlated with circulation patterns, but increased the total 'transactions' by about 2.75 times. Rubin's *In-house use of materials in public libraries*[68] found that if in-house use was measured by counting items left on library tables, the average ratio of items used in the library to items circulated was 0.5 to 1, while patron interviews on the same theme suggested a ratio of 1 to 1. A substantial proportion of patrons – between 47% – 63% – used materials in the library, and whereas most patrons spent less than half an hour in the library, the 'in-house users' spent half an hour or more. Harris reported a survey[264] in Newcastle Polytechnic library in which 8,500 volumes (or 10% of the stock) were studied for a period of 19 months. Fifty per cent received no issues or in-house use in that period, whilst 55% received no issues and 80% received no in-house use.

There are numerous other studies, but the three referred to above are diverse enough in their findings to draw attention to a characteristic problem of user studies: the wide variations in results. Ford summarized his section on in-house use by observing that the ratio of books consulted in-house to books borrowed has been reported as a range from 0.4:1 to 11.2:1. He drew three conclusions. Short-term study of in-house use cannot safely predict long-term patterns. A study in one library cannot safely predict patterns in another. And even within one library there is a wide difference between patterns of use from one subject to another.

Methods of studying in-house use are described both by Ford and by Lancaster, in an informative article.[56] They include direct interviews with users at library exits – the method used in the University of Birmingham study[74] and asking users to complete questionnaires. Both methods rely upon users recalling their library behaviour patterns, and are therefore likely to be inaccurate to some degree. Direct observation seems to be a method that is under-used – surprisingly, since it provides accurate information, especially in a small library or for studying one compact section of a library such as the periodicals collection (for which purpose, Wenger and Childress[75] carried out their research library study).

'Indirect observation' often refers to reshelving surveys, involving counts of items left by users on reading tables – on the assumption that these items were used in-house. The method seems quite popular, and usually seems to reflect the pattern of use whilst seriously underestimating the amount. On a point of library housekeeping, the simple strategem of date stamping items left upon tables is a useful way of keeping some sort of check on the use of reference books.

Availability

Neither circulation nor in-house use studies reveal anything about the failure of users to locate specific items at the shelf, although this information is certainly of interest to the librarian trying to improve the effectiveness of stock. Some of the early work in this area was done in the 1970s by Schofield,[69] who used a simple system of asking users to complete a slip of paper for each 'failure' to locate an item at the shelf. He found the failure rate to be 37%, and identified the 500 titles (out of a shelf stock of half a million) which were most often unavailable. A description of the methods used was later revised and issued by the Centre for Library and Information Management.[42]

Since then a number of availability studies have been carried out – Mansbridge summarizes 40 in his 1986 article.[61] Line[58] has written on the subject in Britain. The best known work has been done by Kantor,[54] who estimates that in large academic lending libraries the probability that specific works will be found when needed is 0.57 (0.66 in a reference library). Revill[298, 299] recently reported availability of 0.69 and 0.75 in a polytechnic library.

Kantor's method for identifying causes of unavailability is generally recognized to be the most accurate, and has been refined to demonstrate linear relationships between various non-availability categories. He has developed five categories for classifying non-availability of individual titles: 1) title not acquired, 2) catalogue error, 3) title in circulation, 4) library error (title missing or misplaced on shelves), and 5) user error in searching. To these might be added 'binding', which in the case of journals is often the most common reason for non-availability.

Non-availability studies have their critics. Schofield pointed out that failures to find are naturally in proportion to the number of successes – one man's success being another's failure. Much depends upon the efficiency of a library's housekeeping, particularly the accuracy of shelving. Also, failure surveys of this kind fail to show up users who do not check the shelves because of low expectation of success. Some critics have suggested that improvement of services will improve success only transitorily, since higher expectations will increase user demand and drag success rates back towards a constant. It is a pity that much of the work done has been linked to specific titles in an academic library setting. Perhaps the most interesting questions relate to subject demand in public libraries, linked to the activity of stock revision.

Survey methods

A variety of different *survey* methods have been touched on above, in describing studies related to circulation, in-house use and availability. Ford gives a useful 'typology' of survey methods, and Line's book *Library surveys: an introduction to their use, planning, procedure and presentation*[59] provides, as the title suggests, a full practical guide to all aspects of the subject.

The most commonly used survey methods are direct observation of user behaviour or direct seeking of user opinions. Opinions may be solicited by asking users to keep diaries on library use over a specific period, by interviewing a sample of users, or by asking users to complete questionnaires. Each carries advantages and disadvantages, and methods must be carefully chosen to relate to situations. Questionnaires, interviews, etc. should be planned with extreme care (a pilot survey is indispensable in almost every circumstance), and must be completed by, administered to, etc. a large enough proportion of the total of users to render the results statistically valid. Finally, it should be clear from the outset what sort of information the survey is designed to elicit.

Some public library authorities have gone beyond user surveys to conduct sociological investigations into their communities, so as to draw inferences about reading habits and information needs. Such studies are often referred to as *community profiles*, and may cover factors such as education, occupation, age, literacy, language (related to ethnic groups), recreation, the needs of the handicapped and housebound, housing and many other matters. Essential reading for anyone intending to compile a community profile are the guidelines offered by Beal[36] and by Jordan and Walley.[53]

6 *Book evaluation*

'Book evaluation' relates to the assessment or appraisal of material. In selection each book, periodical, etc. has to be evaluated individually against a background of other features – library policy, user demand, and so on – before a selection decision can be made. This applies whether books are being ordered new on publication, or during the course of a subject stock revision (see Chapters 8 and 9 respectively).

In this chapter various features which contribute to evaluation are considered separately: certain key characteristics of books themselves, such as price, level and readability; physical characteristics, such as bindings and typefaces; publishers' information about books; reviews; and the impact of reservations. Evaluative bibliographies, which are such an important feature, are considered separately in Chapter 7.

It is worth considering whether an examination of the book itself is necessary to this process of evaluation. In practice many librarians do insist on seeing books before ordering, and the system of obtaining 'on approval' copies through library suppliers is widespread. Often this seems to be taken to unnecessary lengths, since there are relatively few instances where seeing the book helps a selection decision, and even fewer where it is significant. (The subject is discussed at more length on pp.120 – 1). Probably the sensible course is for most books to be ordered sight unseen, with the occasional title requested 'on approval' when it is thought that seeing the book would be helpful.

Key characteristics of materials
Some key characteristics of library materials are now considered, to see how they bear upon a selection decision. In practice these will not all be considered for every title. Often, one feature of

a book will automatically ensure selection – e.g. the reputation of the author, on the appearance of a new work by a famous novelist or an authority on a subject. Or equally, one feature may rule a work out – for instance, the wrong level of content, an unusual format, or a very high price.

Price

Judgement of price is a difficult matter, for it requires an awareness of the pricing structure of publishing which has produced a given price at any given time. The selling price of a book stems principally from the number of copies which are printed, which in turn depends upon the publisher's estimate of the likely demand for the book. For instance, a work of scholarship devoted to an esoteric subject will sell for a significantly higher price than a novel of approximately the same length and format by a popular writer. The same may be true of a book which has been deliberately produced to a high standard of physical appearance.

Identification of new book prices is increasingly a problem for librarians. Prices tend to be omitted from publishers' catalogues (or given in a separate leaflet which becomes detached from the main catalogue). *British national bibliography* entries often omit prices. Prices given in publishers' advance publicity will often have risen, in some cases very considerably, by the time the book appears. Despite these difficulties, it goes without saying that no book should be ordered unless the price is known.

Date

Usually the date of publication may be taken as given, but in a few cases – particularly where publication in book form follows several years after original research – imprint date should be compared against any dates given in the foreword or introduction.

Related to the subject of date is the matter of new editions, and the extent to which the latest edition differs from the previous one. A comparison of the two texts is sometimes enough to establish how many copies of the new edition should be bought, and whether the previous edition should be retained or discarded – though it is a time-consuming process. For research work, references to recent titles in a book's bibliography can be a good indicator of currency in the text.

41

Author

The reputation of the author is often a highly significant characteristic in popular fiction and other general reading. For purposive reading and for textbooks and research material the author's credentials are generally to be found on the title page or in publishers' promotional material. They can establish, at least, that the author is an authority on the subject – though this does not of course necessarily guarantee the quality of the end product.

Publisher

A knowledge of publisher's reputations and known specializations often help in evaluating a book's content. Brief comments on publishers appear on pp.116 – 17.

Level

The level of library material is an important feature in determining its suitability for particular audiences (for instance, undergraduates, postgraduates or researchers in an academic library, or the various user groups served by public libraries). Sweeney[82] and Jones and Pratt[77] have made attempts to produce some basic definitions of level which might be helpful to librarians and users. The latter carried out experiments based on six 'level' categories: 1) compendia, 2) light, popular, 3) serious popularized, 4) elementary, 5) standard (authoritative works and standard factual presentations) and 6) advanced.

McClellan proposed a different series of categories[78] based upon what he called the function of material, rather than level alone. The categories were: prospective (popular and general reader guides to the subject); instructional and structural (for mastery of the principal elements of the subject); bibliography and reference; interdisciplinary and specialist (related fields of knowledge as they bear on the main subject, as in history and sociology); critical and projective (research, innovatory thought).

To date none of the various definitions of level have been widely accepted. A further difficulty, established by the research cited above, is the considerable variation in the way that users and librarians assign given definitions of level to actual materials. It appears to be easier to categorize users than it is to assign levels to books.

Published bibliographies rarely give level indicators, and

publishers' information tends, in this respect, to be unreliable. The author's intentions are probably the most reliable guide, and examination of a book's preface or foreword can give an indication of these.

Readability

A distinction may be observed between 'style' in books of imaginative literature, and 'style' in works where the main purpose is the efficient communication of facts or ideas. Judgement of the former is particularly difficult. The relationship between content and style has been a constant and controversial preoccupation of literary critics. It seems unlikely that many librarians have the time or the flair for effective judgement of style in this sense, and sampling of the text of 'serious' novels or other works of literature is unlikely to prove a worthwhile activity.

In any case for the library user the style of popular books – particularly popular fiction – is often not a preoccupation. It has been observed that two out of three fiction readers in libraries do not look at the text of a book before choosing it.[302] This may in part be due to the similarity of styles used in much of the genre fiction, and the fact that readers' expectations in terms of style are therefore rarely disappointed.

In factual works, style plays a more easily definable role, and textual sampling and attempts at stylistic evaluation by librarians are more pertinent. The selector may try to assess the complexity of the language used, and how this relates to the linguistic experience of his various reader groups, bearing in mind that some subject areas, and the treatment of them, necessarily demand a more complex form of language than others.

As with imaginative literature, readers of factual works are divided between those who find an ill-written work virtually unreadable (probably a fairly small percentage) and those who are largely indifferent to matters of writing style (probably the big majority). Nevertheless it seems sensible for librarians to aim at selecting books which are well-written, where there is a choice. Choice occurs chiefly in the areas of popularizations, introductions to a subject field and textbooks, where badly or unsuitably written texts may be rejected because there are alternatives available. Ranganathan refers to work which is 'written with flair in a simple clear style ...' in 'the latest state of the language'.[296] Any discussion of evaluating style presupposes that librarians are equipped to pass judgement upon such matters. It seems reasonable to suppose that they should be, if the contentious area of imaginative literature is ruled out. Because of a shortage of time most selectors will have to rely upon a quick and subjective sampling technique. As long as the definition of an 'acceptable' style is widely interpreted such an approach is a valid one.

In a great many works of an advanced nature (research material, monographs etc.) style will not play a crucial role, since the content will be unavailable in any other form. The interest and motivation of the reader will normally overcome any deficiencies in the writing, and the librarian need not waste time attempting stylistic assessment.

Another kind of readability affects users who are learning a language (children or foreign language learners) and users with literacy problems. In libraries serving these or similar groups the use of readability formulas may be considered, in which sentence length and word complexity are taken into account to rate the simplicity of the language used. Various readability formulas are described in the course of interesting disquisitions on readability by Hatt[50] and by McClellan.[94] It is doubtful however that many librarians outside language teaching institutions or areas with serious literacy problems will find the time or the need to consult them.

Index, bibliography

The existence of a bibliography and index in a book may be ascertained from its entry in the national bibliography, but the quality of these items is best judged from examination of the book itself. Footnotes and references may reinforce a claim to original research. A good bibliography – particularly if annotated – may reflect an author's authoritative grasp of his field (conversely, a large bibliography of titles listed baldly, without organization or comment, may indicate that an outsider has been employed for its preparation).

The absence of an index limits a book's scope and rules out its use as a reference tool. Ranganathan asserts that releasing a book without an index should be an indictable offence. As in the case of a bibliography, an index may form an integral part of the book, or an extra of dubious value tacked on as an afterthought. The quality of the index should therefore be closely examined. For instance, subdivision under major entries of the index is desirable to ensure that information in the text can be located without delay.

Physical features of books

To what extent is selection influenced by a book's physical features? A well-known publisher, Anthony Blond, writes[246] 'The design and appearance of a general book matters but not too much: after all, printing is only a form of communication and rarely an end in itself. A book should be readable and clean, and the design should not obtrude to the extent that it distracts the reader from the author's thought.' Without doubt, content is the main consideration in most kinds of library, and it is probably rare for physical characteristics to play a decisive role in the selection decision. When they do, it is usually in the public library sphere, where the promotion of reading is an important aspect of service, and where a choice between different works covering the same subject occurs more often – for instance, in the fields of children's books, light fiction, and popular introductions. In academic and special libraries, the information content of books, and the way the content is organized, by far outweigh other considerations (perusal of duplicated or variotyped documents being an occupational penance of the research worker).

Format

Though not a major consideration, format does affect shelf-life and use. Oversized books suffer from the serious disadvantage that they are housed in a separate sequence from the main stock, and are invariably less well used. Pamphlets are unsuitable for open shelf stock. Pocket-sized books are more likely to be stolen. Omnibus editions of novels tend to be too heavy to be read with comfort.

Binding

Publishers' casings are unsuitable for heavy library use, and many public librarians take up various options for strengthened editions offered by the library suppliers. Spiral bindings are inappropriate for library use. Selectors should also avoid books which are so tightly bound that they have to be held forcibly open.

Illustrations

Good photography or colour reproductions can enhance the quality of a book, but are rarely a crucial factor outside the obvious field of the visual arts.

Typography

Standards of typography will rarely be a decisive factor in selection, but there is no doubt that small print is disliked by many readers – including those with good eyesight – and should be avoided on the relatively rare occasions that alternatives are available (for instance, with the different editions of popular classics, or with light fiction, where the choice is very wide and content is less variable).

Publishers' information

The main thing to bear in mind about information distributed by publishers is that it is a form of advertising. It aims to promote, rather than to evaluate, the product. Nevertheless the various kinds of publishers' handouts often give useful information about book *content* and in some cases (notably with forthcoming books) often provide the only available information of any kind.

Most of the larger publishers issue two kinds of list. The complete catalogue, usually annual, gives an author and title record of all books in print from the publisher concerned. In Spring and Autumn, the traditional publishing seasons, lists of forthcoming books with substantial annotations give a good indication of the content of the publisher's output for the next four month period. The Spring and Autumn 'export editions' of *The bookseller* form a sort of abbreviated conglomerate of these catalogues.

The way that this information is used by libraries varies considerably, according to the type of publishers and the type of library. Most libraries try to maintain a comprehensive, updated collection of catalogues as bibliographical checking tools, but many also use them for book selection. A 1979 survey by Malcolm Smith of 'Book selection sources'[301] reported that publishers' information was used for selection purposes by 10% of public libraries, 22% of specialized libraries, and 35% of academic libraries. The figures may have changed a decade later, but the proportions are probably still fairly accurate in showing the more specialized libraries more likely to use publishers' catalogues. It is also probably true that the more specialized the catalogue the more likely it is to be used for selection – for instance, the catalogues of local publishers, those of specialized formats (e.g. microforms, large print books), or those in subject fields which are dominated by the work of one or two publishers.

Selecting from publishers' catalogues throws up at least two knotty practical difficulties. Firstly, the information about price and publication date often proves to be inaccurate when the books appear, because of their inclusion in a catalogue before the final details were known to the publishers themselves. Secondly, there are administrative and logistic problems about selecting from the very large numbers of catalogues available, and many librarians prefer to select from a single bibliographical source (see Chapter 8), cross-checking to publishers' catalogues if more details about particular titles are needed.

Publishers often distribute, in addition to catalogues, circulars about individual books or series. These are quite widely used in special and academic libraries, but are more likely to be consigned to wastepaper baskets in public libraries.

Publishers' blurbs – i.e. the brief descriptions of books on the insides of dust covers – may sometimes be used as selection information by librarians, and are certainly a very important factor for readers selecting from library shelves, though they constitute at best a dubious selection instrument for librarians and readers alike. Anthony Blond's interpretation of blurb cliches[247] strikes the right satirical note: ('Kafkaesque' = 'obscure'; 'frank and outspoken' = 'obscene'; 'well-known' = 'unknown'; 'ingenious' = 'unbelievable'; etc.).

Reservations

To the extent that it indicates demand, receipt of a reservation for a book is a factor influencing the selection decision. Most commonly this happens in the case of a new book, and the reservation merely reminds or forewarns the librarian of the existence of a title which would in any case find its way into stock. Occasionally a reservation is received for an older work missed (or turned down) when originally published. In this case the librarian may choose to purchase or borrow through the interlending system, depending upon the work's quality and the likelihood of its being requested and/or used again.

In academic libraries a large number of requests for a new book may suggest that it is a recommended text, and is likely to influence the number of copies purchased (probably for the short loans collection).

In public libraries, reservation pressure is more volatile, and can – if allowed to – distort the selection process. One large-scale survey in 1979[80] gave a broad picture of reservation demand. Two-thirds of all reservations received were for new books. The majority of requests were for fiction (47%) or popular non-fiction (22%). Only 10% were for advanced material, and another 12% for a category defined as 'standard' works. A second survey of fiction use[302] indicated that most fiction readers did not use the reservation service. Six per cent said they did so 'frequently', 31% 'occasionally', and 62% 'never'. The surveys confirmed what public librarians know from practical experience – that reservation pressure comes mainly from a small minority of users, and mainly for new fiction and non-fiction titles reviewed in the Sunday and daily newspapers. Waiting lists from this sort of reservation pressure can be very substantial indeed – as much as 100 reservations at a single service point in some authorities.

In theory this sort of transitory demand from a minority of the community should not be allowed to influence selection decisions, but in practice librarians have often found it difficult to ignore long waiting lists entirely when selecting new books. Part of the answer to this pressure can lie in centralized monitoring and supply of reservations. There is no need to allocate a copy of a book to a service point which happens to receive one or two reservations for it.

Ultimately the answer to heavy reservation pressure is for selectors to keep their nerve, and refuse to over-provide in a way which will prejudice other elements of the stock used by larger sections of the community.

Reviews

Reviews in the popular press

In the UK, a good deal of space is given to book reviews in the 'serious' daily and Sunday newspapers and in weeklies such as *Spectator* and *New statesman*. The bulk of reviews in these papers cover just a few subject areas. A survey[79] of all reviews appearing in British daily and Sunday newspapers over a period of three months in 1973 reported coverage as follows: fiction (873 reviews); biography (621); children's books (449); art (246); history (242); natural science (129); literature (126); poetry (119); humour (113); politics and economics (102). In contrast, books on education received 7 reviews over the same period, medicine 7, chemistry, mathematics and physics, nil.

The space given to book reviews is relatively generous from the point of view of a newspaper proprietor, but coverage in relation to what is published is (with the exception of fiction) minimal. Anthony Blond analysed[245] the reviews appearing in the three main reviewing Sunday papers in one week, finding totals of 19, 17 and 24 reviews respectively – a fraction of the books published that week. Coverage is further restricted because the same titles tend to crop up in each paper. The choice of book is usually restricted to well-known writers from well-known publishers, reviewed by well-known names.

The reviewers' approach varies. Fiction, for instance, is usually given objective critical treatment. Biographies and political memoirs – to which a lot of space is granted – are often used as a device for the reviewer to express his own prejudices. The readability of the review itself is the paramount editorial consideration. The approach is not particularly useful for public librarians, but then the reviews are not written for librarians. Their main virtue in this respect is their currency, since they provide a pointer to likely public demand (much of it stemming from the reviews themselves). Outside the field of fiction (and possibly, biography), coverage is not wide enough for librarians to use them as a regular source of selection information.

Reviews in specialist journals

For academic and special librarians the most useful reviewing sources are the specialized journals. Most specialized journals contains some book reviews, and there are 'review journals' entirely devoted to reviewing. Reviews in both groups tend to be very full and by authorities on their subjects. Walford's *Reviews and reviewing*[83] surveys specialized sources in a number of subject areas.

Little is known about review coverage in particular subject

49

areas. Grogan has commented,[263] 'Eventually the majority of scientific and medical books do get reviewed at least once, though this is less true of technical books, particularly those of a practical or industrial character'. The main drawback to specialist reviews is their late appearance, often six months to a year after publication of the book to which they refer. Since monographs can go out of print a year after publication, and since the heaviest use of monographs is normally in the year and a half following publication, librarians obviously cannot rely upon reviews as a selection tool.

General reviewing journals

There are a handful of multi-subject reviewing journals, which vary in content and audience. The *Times literary supplement* (*TLS*) is almost an institution in itself, and is unusual in being designed specifically for librarians, although read by large numbers of other people as well. The *TLS* covers about 50 books a week, from most fields except science and technology. Reviews are by experts, mostly very full, and scholarly in approach. The *London review of books* is another serious reviewing journal, of a literary/political nature. Both journals, however, review books well after publication date.

In many ways the *Good book guide* is a useful reviewing tool for public librarians, though it is produced by a bookseller and therefore designed to sell books. However it is current, and its coverage – fiction, biography, travel, hobbies, popular science, etc. – is of subjects which interest the public library's clientele, and which are given little critical attention by other sources.

Summary

Librarians need to know about the main reviewing agencies in their field: their frequency and coverage, the authority and quality of their reviews, the time lags in appearance. But however good the reviewing agencies are, there are likely to be three major problems about using them. The review coverage, when measured against the total number of books of interest to the library, will be inadequate. Delays in appearance of the reviews will mean that librarians must make selection decisions before they appear. And the reviews which are published will often be difficult to trace.

With rare exceptions therefore (the selection of fiction may be one) librarians will not normally wait for reviews before selecting books. But most do still read reviews, usually as a form of long-stop to make sure they have not missed important titles on their initial selection, or to buy extra copies of titles which have been particularly well received.

Even when reviews do exist, tracking them down for a particular title can be difficult. If the book is a new one, then only a homemade index of reviews following scanning of newspapers or journals is likely to be effective. For the purposes of stock revision, back files of reviewing journals (accessed through their indexes) can be extremely useful. There are also some general tools for locating reviews retrospectively, but they are mostly American in coverage. The *Book review index*[249] does include a number of British journals (but not British newspapers).

7 Bibliographies

Bibliographies are the most important sources of information for book selection, and a close understanding of their functions is essential – especially for stock revision. Librarians must be able to interpret the value of each bibliography, its authority, its currency, and its relevance to the work in hand.

No attempt is made in this book to give a comprehensive listing of important bibliographies. The main sources are laid out in Brian Baumfield's chapter in the *Manual of library economy*,[85] and there are also various listings of bibliographies, of which the sections in Walford's *Guide to reference material*[309] are particularly well known. The purpose of this chapter is to distinguish between the main types of bibliography used for selection, and to give a few pertinent examples of each.

National bibliographies
A national bibliography normally serves several purposes. Butcher's lucid paper[87] describes the three main functions of the *British national bibliography* (*BNB*) – viz., a national bibliographic reference service, an aid to current book selection, and a source of catalogue and file records for those libraries which acquire the books themselves. In most developed countries the national bibliography entries are available in machine-readable form – as, for instance, with UK MARC records. This is an important point, since in many libraries selection is part of an integrated approach which also includes acquisition and cataloguing, and the national bibliography's machine-readable records are used for all these functions (although the actual selection process is usually based upon the print version). In fact a common complaint over the past decade has been that the high level of data content included in entries for the benefit of cataloguing records has been

achieved at the cost of timeliness, and the *BNB* has certainly lost ground as a selection source for this reason. Nevertheless it is probably still the most effective selection tool for new books, because of its comprehensiveness and the detail of its content.

The matter of timeliness is discussed, in relation to the selection decision for new books, in Chapter 8. An important factor here is the UK Cataloguing-in-Publication programme (CIP), which provides pre-publication information for a large proportion of the new titles.

A 1985 survey by Bishop and Lewis[243] threw some light on the way that *BNB* was actually used in UK libraries. Of the 170 public, academic and other libraries surveyed, 91% used *BNB* for checking bibliographical references, 77% for book selection and acquisition, 77% for subject searching, and 48% for obtaining cataloguing data. (Of the alternative tools used for selection, the most popular were *The bookseller* with 31%, and publishers' lists with 28%.) Another table showed the level of satisfaction with *BNB* for various reasons, graded from 1 (very dissatisfied) to 5 (very satisfied). All functions scored reasonable marking between 3 and 4, but book selection and acquisition obtained the lowest average marking at 3.14 – the main reasons for dissatisfaction being given as lack of currency, inaccuracy of cataloguing-in-publication data, and lack of comprehensiveness.

Despite these complaints – which to a large extent were valid comments on *BNB* at the time of the survey – the main advantages of national bibliographies as selection tools relate to two of the factors mentioned. A national bibliography like *BNB* does aim to be *comprehensive* in coverage, within certain stated limits, of which the selector must be aware (for instance, *BNB* is not comprehensive for government publications, which must therefore be trawled in other listings). Of course, even within the stated parameters, comprehensiveness is an impossible goal, because some publications escape the net, or are listed so late that they have gone out of print or are out-of-date by the time they appear. Nevertheless, a bibliography such as *BNB* is as comprehensive a listing as can be found, and is therefore used by many librarians as a base selection tool, to ensure that all new publications are at least considered for selection. See Chapter 8 on the advantages of using a single base selection tool rather than a number of different sources.

The second main advantage of national bibliographies as selection tools is the *detail of entry* given. This is not to say that the detail is ideal. Apart from the matter of inaccuracies, mentioned above, there are other factors which hinder selection decisions. Descriptive annotations are not normally given. There is no specific indication of level. There is no evaluation of content.

Nevertheless a close inspection of entries in – for instance – *BNB*, shows that in fact a good deal of information is contained there. Subjects are closely defined, both by classification numbers and by the system of feature headings used, through which the subject is pinpointed by increasingly specific descriptors. The treatment and level of the material is often apparent from the information given, which includes the publisher and date, the series entry, the sub-title, pagination, the existence of illustrations, bibliography and index. For many new titles the scope of the book will be readily apparent from these details alone, and selection can be made without reference to other sources.

Trade listings
The second new title listing which aims at comprehensiveness is the trade listing. An example of this is the UK listing *The bookseller* – 'the organ of the book trade'. As the sobriquet implies, this is principally used by booksellers for acquisition and as a finding list, but it is also used by some librarians for selection purposes. Like the *BNB* it aims at completeness, and includes large and small publishers alike. It is also ideal if currency is required, since it normally lists new titles in the same month as publication. A paper by David Whitaker[87] claims an 86% hit rate for *Bookseller* entries with public libraries at the time of ordering titles, and 80% – 100% hit rates at the time of cataloguing. As with many trade listings, *Bookseller* entries are available in many formats – print, microfiche, tape and CD-ROM (the last particularly useful, when searched under title keywords, for stock revision purposes).

The obvious disadvantage of trade listings is the limited detail in entries, which tends to be too sparse to support a reliable selection decision. Also, the alphabetical author/title arrangement is less helpful than the usual classified sequence of national bibliographies.

Subject bibliographies

Subject bibliographies are the most valuable tools available for stock revision purposes. The key requirement is that they should be *selective*, which suggests that an authority on the subject has sifted through the literature and identified the most important books, periodicals, etc. Ideally, each entry will carry an annotation which is both informative and *evaluative* (that is, critical, or making an appraisal). A good selective bibliography gives a bird's eye view of the subject literature, and where a reliable source of this kind already exists, stock revision in the subject area is considerably simplified. Instead of needing to evaluate each title in the field personally, librarians may select from an already select list. What is mainly required thereafter is to verify the authority and reliability of the list itself, and to update the content by evaluating works which have appeared since its publication.

Subject bibliographies are therefore the raw materials of the trade of stock revision, and librarians working on stock revision should seek to acquire a working knowledge of their existence and contents in the same way that a reference librarian is familiar with the major reference tools in the collection.

R. Benge, in a valuable discussion of select bibliographies,[86] notes that this kind of listing offers various degrees of helpfulness to its user:

1.   Lists in which items appearing are selected, and purport to be the most important works on the subject, but for which no annotation, evaluative or informative, is given.
2.   Lists where use of symbols is made to give informative or evaluative comment on the content of titles.
3.   Lists in which an evaluative or informative annotation is given for each item.
4.   Critical reviewing agencies in which detailed individual evaluations are made of each title.

Librarianship textbooks sometimes draw a distinction between 'select bibliographies' and 'guides to the literature', defining the latter as providing a discussion of the structure of the subject literature and bibliographical examples, rather than a full set of references. Denis Grogan's *Science and technology: an introduction to the literature*[263] is an outstanding example. In practice it is often difficult to define bibliographical types in a way that gives a reliable guide to content, and the selector is best advised to look at each bibliography individually. Reading a work's introduction can be helpful, though even then content may not live up to the billing, so that a sampling of the text is also advised. A few examples of bibliographies are noted below, with brief comments on their type and function:

1. Walford, A. J. *Guide to reference material.* 3 vols. Library Association, Vol. 1, 5th ed, 1989. Vol. 2, 4th ed, 1982. Vol. 3, 4th ed, 1987.
A fine model for a select bibliography, wide-ranging in coverage, yet highly selective. With critical annotations which often compare the items with other, similar titles. Widely used for revising reference stock in all types of library.

2. Brown, L. M. and Christie, I. R. *A bibliography of British history 1789 – 1851.* Oxford University Press, 1979.
One of a series of select bibliographies on British history. Despite the editorial policy of being 'ruthlessly selective', it contains over 5,000 items, many of them now out of print. Ideal, say, for a university library building up stock – particularly if secondhand wants lists were being compiled – though someone revising the history stock at a small public library service point would look for a more selective tool.

3. Wood, D. N. and others. *Information sources in the earth sciences.* Bowker-Saur, 2nd ed, 1989.
One of the extensive and valuable 'Guide to information sources' series (previously published by Butterworths) exploring the literature of pure and applied sciences and the social sciences. The approach varies from title to title, or even within one volume when different chapters are by different hands, but nearly all titles in the series list the major works in all aspects of their subject, often in discursive critical sections, giving liberal examples.

4. Hall, J. L. and Brown, M. J. *On-line bibliographic databases.* Aslib, 3rd ed, 1983.
This work has established itself as a bibliography of a single format, in a rapidly growing field. Very much a select bibliography, as the introduction makes clear, since it attempts to list the most important databases from the much larger number available. Extensive annotations.

5. *CD-ROM directory, 1989*. TFPL, 1988.
Another bibliography of a single format, in a still faster growing field. This is not a selective bibliography, since the authors write that they ' . . . have tried to track down all available products . . .' (though they are unlikely to have succeeded).

6. Prytherch, R. *Sources of information in librarianship and information science*. Gower, 2nd ed, 1987.
A title in the 'guide to the literature' mode, since it outlines the structure of the subject literature and gives examples, but does not attempt comprehensive listings of works. For students of librarianship, rather than for stock revision.

7. *Children's books of the year*. Andersen Press, annual.
A highly selective bibliography produced by the Book Trust, which annually attempts to choose the best children's books for a range of ages. Highly suitable for a small children's collection with modest funds for annual updating of stock.

8. *Waterstone's guide to books*. Waterstone, 2nd ed, 1988.
This list's provenance should be carefully noted, since it comes from a retail bookseller, and is therefore intended primarily to sell books. Nevertheless it is an immensely useful selective bibliography covering fields where few such lists exist – fiction, biography, travel, hobbies, etc. Contains 60,000 'in print' titles. Very suitable for public library stock revision.

9. Watson, G. (ed.) *The concise Cambridge bibliography of English literature 600 – 1950*. Cambridge University Press, 2nd ed, 1965.
A famous selective bibliography. No annotations. Contrast with the even more famous 5-volume *New Cambridge bibliography of English literature*, also by Cambridge University Press, which aims at 'completeness in its own terms' – i.e. excluding certain categories of works (such as unpublished dissertations) – but otherwise attempting comprehensiveness. Both works were published two decades ago, and need to be supplemented by evaluation of more recent literature.

Pamphlet bibliographies
Many of the numerous pamphlet bibliographies published each year are useful for stock revision purposes – particularly in very specific, discrete subject areas. Tracing these lists can be a major

problem. Some of the most valuable ones do not themselves appear in other listings, and can often be found only through the institution that produced them (the importance of organizations being a recurrent theme in subject bibliography). Amongst important sources are the following:

1. Any organization concerned with the promotion of books, such as the Book Trust, the Book Development Council of the Publishers Association, or the British Council. (The British Council publishes the monthly journal *British book news*, which contains invaluable bibliographical survey of different subjects.)

2. Official bodies, organizations and societies of all kinds which publish select bibliographies in their own subject field for the benefit of their members. They include advisory bodies and quangos, consumer and welfare associations, tourist agencies, research associations, professional institutions, trade organizations, hobby and interest societies.

3. Catalogues and lists from libraries specializing in one subject.

4. Lists distributed by reputable specialist bookshops.

5. Some publishers' catalogues – e.g. local publishers, publishers who monopolize a particular subject field, and publishers of special formats (e.g. large print books, microforms).

Reading lists and bibliographies in books

Valuable bibliographic information is to be found in the reading lists of reference books and standard works. In fact for some subject areas these are the only form of bibliographical support available. They vary greatly in length, scope, selectivity and reliability, and must be carefully evaluated in relation to the stock revision in progress. The more selective bibliographies – such as those in 'lists for further reading' – are often more useful than the sort of lengthy, unclassified bibliographies which give no clue to the standing of individual items. (On occasion, the latter are produced on commission, and bear little relevance to the contents of the book.) It is worth photocopying the more useful reading lists, and filing them in classified order in a pamphlet bibliography collection.

Reviews of progress

'Reviews of progress' are a special form of research bibliography which commonly appear in series at intervals of one or more years, and which distil the literature of that period. A kind of intermediary synthesis of information before its eventual distillation into the monograph form, they contain extensive references to books, reports, periodical articles, etc., and are often given titles such as *Advances in . . .* or *Progress in . . . .* A good example from the field of librarianship is the Library Association's series *British librarianship and information work*, of which the last edition covered the years 1981 – 5. On occasion, the literature survey may be restricted to one chapter of a volume – see, for instance, the annual *Shakespeare survey.*

Automated bibliographical searching

The Bishop and Lewis survey[243] already mentioned suggested that in 1985 few librarians used the database *BLAISE-LINE* for selection or stock revision purposes, and many seemed unaware of its possibilities for selection. *BLAISE-LINE* is now just one of a number of bibliographical databases available, and it is likely that this medium will increasingly be used for some aspects of stock revision, as librarians become more familiar with its potential.

Databases which list books usually aim to be comprehensive in their chosen field, rather than selective or evaluative. This has both advantages and disadvantages for selection. The absence of an evaluative element is a limitation for anyone trying to select between different items, but it is helpful to have access to comprehensive lists of titles which can be searched by a variety of subject approaches, especially since these include recent titles which are unlikely to appear in published bibliographies. In practice selectors will use both databases and select bibliographies (assuming the latter are available) so as to take advantage of the best features of both.

Selectors now have a choice of bibliographical databases which can be used for selection. Four prominent British tools, described below, indicate the range of available formats and types of content which can be adapted for different requirements.

BLAISE-LINE is the British Library's online bibliographic service, containing over six million records in a number of databases covering books, periodicals, government publications, report literature, antiquarian material, and non-book material.

Subject approaches may be made through classification numbers, subject headings or keywords.

One of the databases on *BLAISE-LINE* is the Whitaker file, which can be cross-checked against other files to verify if titles are in print. Whitakers also produce this in-print listing of books in the form of a CD-ROM called *BOOK BANK*. Searches may be made through subject headings (though these are too broad to be really useful), or more effectively – at least in the pure and applied sciences – through keywords or combinations of keywords in the titles of books listed.

Bookdata is a new commercial service, which sells bibliographical records tailored to user profiles, giving fuller annotations than most other sources. The variety of subject search approaches and output formats should ultimately make this a valuable service – although to realize full potential it must achieve a more comprehensive coverage of publishers than at present. *Bookdata* records are now available on CD-ROM.

Finally some library suppliers have built up databases of books which can be addressed online by library clients. These can be substantial – one, at least, reaches over a million entries – but they appear to have no obvious advantage over the databases described above, except, perhaps, when they afford the prospect of immediate supply from stock of titles held in their files.

8 *Selecting new books*

Sources and timing

Most libraries spend the bulk of their funds on 'new books' – that is, books purchased on, or shortly before, or shortly after their publication date. Chapters 6 and 7 have looked at the way that books can be evaluated, and at the sources for evaluation. The present chapter examines the timing of the order for new books in relation to sources.

In practice it is relatively rare for all the different sources to be taken into account before an order. Many books almost select themselves, and many others are rejected without any need for a lengthy appraisal process. For instance in a university library a new work of research in a subject relevant to the university's research interests is sure to be ordered, whatever the book's subsequent reception by reviewers, or its physical format, or (within bounds) its price. The only decision to be made is the number of copies, which no doubt rests as much upon the price of the book and the size of the university's bookfund as upon quality factors.

Nonetheless there are titles for which more than one source of information needs to be consulted – either because the titles are borderline choices, and/or because one source does not give all the information needed. Unfortunately, the sources of information do not all appear at the same time. Publishers' announcements and lists from library suppliers usually come a month or two in advance of publication. The appearance of the book itself is followed shortly by its appearance in a book trade listing. Then come other listings, including the national bibliography (though see below for cataloguing-in-publication information), and reviews. During the whole of this period, readers' reservations may be received.

It is important that selection decisions are timed at the right moment in this chain. But when is 'the right moment'? In one sense a later decision is more convenient, because it allows all useful information to be collated, and is more likely to lead to a considered expenditure of funds. But there are several pressures towards making early decisions. The most intensive use of monographs and research material in university and special libraries is in the year immediately after publication – an argument for getting new books onto the shelves quickly. The considerable impact of reservation pressure in public libraries has been noted. The possibility of a title going 'out of print' if selection decisions are delayed must also be considered – though this is unlikely if orders are placed within a few months of publication.

On timing matters, another important point must be considered, viz. that most new book orders should be based upon a single base source. The base source need not be used unsupported. Once it has listed a title, other sources can be used to cast additional light upon the book before a selection decision is reached. But the principle of pinning selection to a single source in this way ensures efficiency. Moreover in any organization with a large number of service points – for instance, a public library authority – use of a base selection source also allows coordination of the acquisition and cataloguing processes.

The alternative to a base source is to consider a variety of different sources at different times, selecting titles as and when they are listed. Though by no means uncommon, this approach wastes a great deal of staff time (because the same titles will be listed and considered in several different sources) and is also likely to lead to duplicate ordering.

Pre-publication selection

A good deal of pre-publication (or 'advance') ordering takes place in all kinds of library. The ultimate in this line is the standing order, usually employed for annuals, which tend to go out of print very quickly once advance subscriptions are satisfied. Advance orders are sometimes placed for all the titles in a particular series, though this is more dubious, not only because titles in a series vary, but because suppliers tend to overlook volumes which come out at prolonged and irregular intervals. Another common advance ordering practice is that of selecting books a few months before publication, after scrutiny of information provided by library suppliers or (in the case of academic libraries) by specialized alerting services which have been set up for this purpose.

A practical objection to pre-publication orders, from an 'acquisitions' point of view, is that they clog up order files and complicate the order process – particularly when titles which have been announced are not actually published. But the main concern must be whether the selection process itself is effective. Sometimes, as observed above, a book virtually selects itself (for instance – in public libraries – the memoirs of a prominent public figure), and if accurate advance information is available then early ordering of such titles is probably sensible. Without sufficient information, a selection decision should be delayed until the book has appeared. And the decision on timing should not be based – as it sometimes is in public libraries – upon reservation pressure from a small minority of the library's clientele.

Selection near to date of publication

Most books are ordered on or around publication date, and here a variety of different tools can be used as a base source. The most common are information from library suppliers (including 'on approval' copies of the books), publishers' information, trade listings and national bibliographies.

The use of on approval copies and of information from library suppliers is increasingly common, though it carries the major disadvantage of leaving the selection process to commercial organizations whose main aim is to make money (see pp.118 – 21).

Publishers' catalogues are often used by university and special librarians. They appear well in advance of publication, and usually contain a good deal of information about individual titles – though here again the information is put together by the producers, who are naturally keen to sell their product. The main problem about this option is the logistic one of getting together the hundreds of different catalogues (especially those of the small publishers) necessary to ensure comprehensiveness.

The advantages of trade listings are discussed on p.54. The timing of the information release is ideal – usually just after publication date – but the amount and presentation of information is less than helpful.

National bibliographies are considered as selection tools on pp.52 – 4. These are in many ways ideal, since they aim at comprehensiveness, are arranged in classified order, and give a good deal of information with each entry. Also, they often provide automated bibliographical records which match libraries' acquisition and cataloguing systems. The *timing* of the appearance of books in national bibliographies is however often a problem.

Timeliness has until recently (see below) been a serious defect of *British national bibliography* (*BNB*) entries. In the case of *BNB*, timeliness is closely allied to the UK Cataloguing-in-Publication programme (CIP), which was begun by the British Library in 1977. Its purpose was to provide pre-publication information which could be used for book selection and acquisition, and subsequently for catalogue records, prior to the creation of a fuller, more authoritative entry – the CIP revised entry. CIP complicates matters of selection considerably because it only relates to some *BNB* entries, and therefore requires that CIP and non-CIP entries must be treated differently. Also, CIP entries have until recently contained less information and less accurate information than other entries.

Many of these problems have been resolved by the recent expansion and improvement of CIP, which has increased the coverage of the scheme to 14,000 titles per annum and rendered CIP entries themselves more accurate. At the same time, currency of non-CIP entries has improved, since they are now listed on average about two months after publication date.

9 *Stock revision*

The previous chapter describes how books are selected at or near their publication date. It is essential that a thorough selection trawl of new books is made, because important titles must be put into stock before they have a chance to go out of print, and because the first year or two after publication is the time that books are usually in most demand. In practice most libraries spend most of their money in this way. Even so, it remains an inefficient way of spending funds, because in considering large numbers of new books on different subjects at the same time selectors find it difficult to judge the quality of individual works in relation to the rest of the subject literature, and difficult to take into account – except in the most superficial way – user demand for the books' subjects.

A much more cost-effective way of spending bookfunds is through stock revision. The selector takes each subject field separately, scrutinizes the library's existing stock on the subject, and the pattern of use, weeds out titles which are out-of-date or unused, studies the structure of the literature and its bibliography, identifies the most important and appropriate works in print, and then selects. By systematically studying use, stock revision ensures that the titles selected relate to demand. By surveying the whole subject literature at once, it ensures that the 'best' and most appropriate titles are purchased in large numbers (and that undeserving titles are not purchased at all).

Finding a proper match between new book selection and stock revision is difficult, if not impossible, because the two approaches are so different. In one sense, new book selection is a way of filling in or updating between stock revisions, but this assumes that the whole of a stock is updated, subject by subject, over a limited timespan, and because stock revision is a highly staff-intensive process that is rarely the case. Looking at things the other way around, it might seem that if selection of new books could be carried out thoroughly, taking proper account of demand, and if proper weeding and replacement procedures could be instituted, stock revision would not be necessary at all. However in practice deterioration of stock inevitably sets in, through a variety of factors: original errors or omissions in selection (for the reasons suggested above); poor control of withdrawals and replacements; fluctuations in funding over a period of years; fluctuations in demand caused by changes in the constituency, or changes in their needs.

Little stock revision is carried out in academic libraries, partly because it is less appropriate for research collections, and partly because few academic libraries pay close attention to the use of stock. Even in public libraries, remarkably little stock revision takes place. Figures are hard to come by, but the recent report *Trends in public library selection policies*[13] notes that 12 out of the 32 libraries surveyed kept 'some' information about allocations for stock revision (suggesting that the remainder did not have any formal programmes of revision). Personal investigation suggests that few public library authorities spend more than 15% of their bookfunds on stock revision, while many spend a good deal less – and most of what is spent goes on fiction, where revision is a relatively straightforward process. Library managements might plead that there is no time for a highly staff-intensive activity such as stock revision, but the low priority given to an activity of such fundamental importance is disconcerting. A personal view, for what it is worth, is that most British public libraries would benefit from spending at least 40% of their bookfunds on stock revision. This will only happen if management allocates specifically to the activity, and subsequently ensures that it is carried out.

Stock revision practice
In practice stock revision may be divided into four stages:

1. Choice and definition of subject
2. Weeding, and examination of existing stock
3. Bibliographical survey of the subject (independent of existing stock)
4. Ordering.

66

Choice and definition of subject

The librarian should normally plan a long-term programme of stock revisions over a period of, say, one to three years, selecting a number of specified priority subjects to be revised during that period. A careful record should be maintained of the subjects completed so that future revision plans can follow a pattern which takes past work into account. This is especially necessary in dealing with large subject areas where – as often happens – only a part of the subject may be revised.

The choice of stock revision subjects depends upon a number of factors, foremost among these being the importance of the different subjects to the library's objectives. This in turn normally reflects the amount of use received by materials in those subjects. A second important factor, affected by the above, is the quality of the existing stock. Sections which fall below an acceptable standard in terms of quantity, quality of content, or physical condition should receive priority. Obviously one influence here is the length of time that has elapsed since that part of the stock was last revised.

Both of these important factors – the amount of use and the quality of existing stock – can be worked out in a formal way if the McClellan system of stock logistics is adopted (see Chapter 10). Even some form of simplified logistics involving issue and shelf counts can provide useful information to guide the choice of subject areas.

Two other minor aspects may influence matters. First, the subject expertise of the staff may be taken into account and made use of where possible. Secondly, the appearance of a good new subject bibliography, appropriate to the library's stock, may signal the moment for stock revision to take place. The bibliographical survey is the longest part of the whole process, and a readily available and up-to-date bibliography can save a good deal of staff time.

Once subject areas have been decided upon, the librarian needs to fix precise boundaries for revision purposes. This is not always as easy as it sounds. A block of classification numbers usually appears to provide fairly precise demarcation lines (though even here the inconsistencies of classification schemes may lead to some difficulties – undesirable elements turning up in an otherwise homogenous subject block). Once stage three gets underway, however, the librarian finds that bibliographies of the subject tend to cut across classification boundaries with impunity, particularly in the humanities and social sciences, and a too rigid adherence to classification numbers means that a good deal of the material which is not easily pigeon-holed can escape the selection net. This is one good reason for planning a long-term programme of revision incorporating a number of subject areas. In practice the librarian must eventually fix some parameters to each revision subject, but should keep them flexible to take account of this problem.

Although an expert knowledge of the subject being revised is obviously an advantage, it is not essential. But a grasp of the subject's structure and its relationship to other subjects should be acquired before the literature is approached. Some preliminary reading may therefore be necessary. A guide to the literature, if one is available, should serve this purpose well, by linking a presentation of the subject to its bibliography.

Weeding and examination of existing stock

The second stage involves working at the library shelves. This falls into two parts. First, weeding of existing stock. Second, examining the stock and gathering information on the pattern of use so that this can be used later at the ordering stage.

Weeding may be considered first. The criteria employed for the weeding process are discussed at some length in Chapter 11. The practice is along the following lines. The librarian goes to the subject area at the shelves and examines each book in sequence, taking account of its physical condition, its currency, and the amount of use it has received. As the work proceeds she/he makes tentative decisions on what to do with each title, and in doing so obviously takes into account the amount of money shortly to be used for replenishing the stock. While making these decisions she/he may also need to consult the library catalogue from time to time – although a main purpose of stock revision is to improve the range of stock available *on the shelves*, as well as titles simply listed in the catalogue. The librarian will need to work with close access to *Books in print*. Where uncertain about a title (particularly those in unfamiliar subject fields) she/he will need to consult selective and evaluative bibliographies for an authoritative opinion before making a final decision.

After a section has been weeded, those books which are considered worth retaining in their existing form will remain on the shelves – one would hope, a substantial proportion. Additionally, there would be various piles of books taken off the shelves and marked for action of one kind or another. These fall into a number of categories.

1. For withdrawal
2. For withdrawal and replacement by same edition
3. For withdrawal and replacement by new edition
4. For binding
5. For cleaning and repair
6. For moving to reserve stock or store
7. For moving from lending to reference stock (or vice versa)
8. For reclassification (if dubiously classified and unused)
9. For further checking pending a decision.

After the shelves have been weeded, all other books which are on loan from that section at the time of weeding should be screened on their return and subjected to the same process. This is especially necessary where a high proportion of the stock of a library is on loan.

Weeding is one function of this stage of work at the shelves. During the weeding process a second function is also carried out, in which the librarian notes the patterns of use and records these for future consultation at the ordering stage. Two perspectives are required. First, he must be aware of the overall strength of use of the section being revised, compared with other sections of the library. Second, within the revised section he should know the degree of use received by different subject elements. Subsequently these variations will be translated into different degrees of emphasis in ordering.

Also during this process he should begin to note down (on cards) details of specific titles that are heavily used and may require duplication. It is a particular advantage of stock revision that titles which have been sparingly ordered originally (probably shortly after publication, when the quality and demand for the book would be largely unknown) can be later duplicated, or triplicated, after a proper study of the demand.

Throughout the second stage, attention should be paid to the reference as well as lending stock. There may be a need for transfer of the stock from one to the other, or for duplication for both sections of titles which are only held in one.

Bibliographical survey
The third stage of stock revision is a comprehensive bibliographical survey of the subject. Its purpose is to discover what is both worthwhile in the literature and available (either in print or obtainable secondhand) and the exercise is carried out independently of existing library stock. Ultimately, ordering will be based upon titles identified during this survey.

This is the most difficult and time-consuming stage of the work, and its effectiveness depends upon making good use of bibliographies, whether these are printed or held on databases. The value of different kinds of bibliography for stock revision purposes is discussed in Chapter 7.

Some practical points are worth noting. Titles which are identified as possible purchases need to be noted down during the course of the stock revision. This may be done manually on cards, but it is probably more efficient to mark up a print-out (taken from a comprehensive database) of all the titles in print in that subject area. For best results the main subject should be subdivided on the print-out into smaller subject fields.

At this stage the selector should note down as much information as possible against each title, including the reason it was marked as a possible purchase – because recommended in a select bibliography, for instance, or as a replacement for a much-used copy on the shelves – and perhaps some form of starring system to identify titles thought to be outstanding of their kind.

Once this process is complete, the titles need to be subdivided into smaller subject areas, so that the selector obtains a bird's-eye-view of the literature of each sub-field. If the information is on cards, the cards can be shuffled accordingly. If titles have been marked on a print-out they should already be subdivided, as suggested above, though some further editing may be necessary.

Ordering
Ordering is the final stage, and if the previous steps have been thoroughly done it is the easiest. Equipped with notes on the use of existing stock, together with a record of the best published works available, the librarian may now decide which titles to add to stock.

The aim is to ensure not only that all important titles are held in stock, but also that as far as possible there is *on the shelves* at any one time a reasonable coverage of material in all subject fields. A single order may not be sufficient for this latter aim, and it is advisable to go back to the shelves some months after the new stock has reached them and decide whether a further order is necessary. The amount of funding available determines how far this process can be taken.

The extent to which subject coverage on the shelves can be achieved is a matter of library policy, funding, the amount of shelf space available, and the efficiency of interlending systems to which the authority has recourse. These influences are considered in more detail in Chapter 12. The case for immediate shelf representation in a public library is made at some length by Ranganathan, in his fourth library law – 'save the time of the reader'. 'Mental hunger for books is not compelling in the case of most people. Mental thirst for information is not inexorable in the case of most people. Both of them are fleeting in their nature. They both die out, unless satisfied immediately on their taking shape. No time lag should come between demand and supply. The tempo for reading is often momentary. It should be harnessed at the very moment.'

Clearly subject coverage is a matter of degree, and no public librarian (nor any reasonable library user) would expect to find works of a very specialized nature immediately available on the shelves of a small service point. On the other hand certain subjects at certain levels (introductory and standard works) *should* always be represented.

Unfortunately public librarians know very little at present about users' success (or lack of it) in searching for particular subjects. Such research as has been done is touched upon in Chapter 5.

Location of copies
Where the selector is dealing with a single service point the final order is a relatively simple operation. Where a number of service points are involved – as they would be in a centrally organized stock revision for a public library authority – the choice of locations for titles ordered is an additional complication. The following factors should be taken into account.

Geography Some consideration should be given, within a very large authority, to spacing out orders geographically. Many readers possess their own forms of transport and are prepared to travel reasonable distances within the authority when requiring material urgently.

Security Safe locations are to be preferred for expensive and/or specialized works or for titles of which only one or two copies are purchased. Service points which have acquired a reputation for losing books – whether through their own or their public's machinations – are to be avoided.

Size of service point The most obviously appropriate locations for specialized material are large service points, where the catchment area is larger and where special collections are sometimes established. An alternative policy is to place some specialized works at small service points where, although their potential use is much smaller, they give the public some indication of the full range of stock available in the authority. This is particularly valid in those authorities which do not carry union catalogues at small service points.

Stock-taking

The term 'stock-taking' refers to a physical check carried out on the bookstock to ensure that the library still actually has all of the items listed in its catalogue or shelf register. Until recently it was not uncommon for a librarian in a public or academic library to carry out an annual check of the entire stock in this way. In the 1980s stock-taking has become a more unfashionable activity and many libraries check their stock rarely or not at all – despite the opportunities for more streamlined stock-taking offered by automated stock records. 'No stock-taking' policies are adopted partly because of staffing shortages, but also on the premise that stock-taking is a waste of time because it does not bring back the missing books, and any item which is really important will be requested on reservation (though a central reservation system, if employed, may mean that missing titles go unnoticed).

The practical result of such policies is an increasingly inefficient system of book provision, leading gradually to an inadequate stock. 'Losses' and thefts from stock normally affect books which are most in demand. Only a fraction of readers make regular use of the reservation service. The remainder are bound to be increasingly affected by the absence from the shelves of a considerable number of titles. The librarian continues to base selection and stock revision programmes on catalogue records which are no longer accurate, and wastes a good deal of time searching for books which are no longer in circulation.

Stock revision programmes offer an alternative to a comprehensive stock-taking. In the course of stock revision the librarian may undertake to check on the physical existence and physical condition of all the items in the catalogue within the subject. In a public library authority this can require all titles from all service points to be called in to a central point and their condition checked and compared. Once the missing items are identified and the true content of the whole authority's stock has been verified, the selection of new and replacement titles can proceed on a more reliable basis. The catalogue is subsequently amended.

10 *Stock logistics*

In the practical work connected with stock provision librarians must come to grips with two fundamentally different activities – both of which are essential to achieve an effective bookstock. Firstly, they must decide how many titles each library should stock on each subject, how to modify these figures as the type of use changes, and how to keep the stock in each subject relatively fresh and interesting. Secondly, having collated this information, they must find a way of translating it into actual literature. The first approach considers the needs in subject and quantitative terms of the users of particular libraries – without any relation to book titles. The second functions from the point of view of the literature itself, and tries to fit actual titles into the 'need' slots on the shelves. A. W. McClellan, whose writings on this subject are indispensable reading,[93, 94] refers to the first of these approaches as 'logistic' and the second as 'bibliographical'. The latter is no less important than the former, and if bibliographical decisions are made wrongly no amount of logistic information can redeem the situation. By the same token, bibliographical decisions must be based – in an efficient system – upon a continuous flow of logistic information.

McClellan's system has been used successfully as the foundation for provision at his former authority of Tottenham Public Libraries, and a handful of authorities still use those ideas today in modified form. McClellan's is the most sophisticated approach yet designed towards solving these logistic problems. It is therefore described below in some detail.

The basis of the McClellan system is the subdivision of the bookstock – for selection and revision purposes – into categories of manageable size, within which both logistic and bibliographical decisions can be made more easily. He calls these 'interest categories', each one intended to represent a discrete field of user interest. Most of the categories in McClellan's suggested list[275] correspond to Dewey classes or groups of Dewey classes. The intention is to achieve categories within which the size of the *shelf* stock at any service point is no more than 100 titles.

The first requirement of the system is for the librarian at each service point to estimate the desired *size* of his stock *on the shelves* for each interest category. To this end he makes periodic counts, from the issue records, of the number of books on loan in each category. He then needs to estimate the desired shelf stock size for each category on the basis of this record of use. It would seem at first sight feasible to calculate this size in a way which reflected precisely the actual use for each category. This could be achieved by totalling the loan counts for each interest category and then expressing each count as a percentage of the total. To do so, however, would be to ignore the awkward problem of adequate representation for minority interests. Library use is never evenly distributed throughout the stock, and it is accepted that some stock categories will only be used by a small number of readers. At the same time the appetite of those few readers for books in their category will not necessarily be any smaller than that of readers in a large interest category. Some form of adjustment is therefore required to give users in minority interest categories a 'better deal'. McClellan's 'square root' principle offers a mathematical solution to the problem which, though crude, has not yet been supplanted by an alternative. Using the count of books on loan at a given time for each interest category, he takes the square root of each of these numbers. Then

> the square roots obtained from all the interest category loan components are totalled and then each individual square root is calculated as a percentage of that total. The shelf stock for each interest category is calculated by expressing its loan component percentage as a percentage of the total open shelf capacity of the library. The effect of this method of arriving at desirable proportions between the categories is to introduce a controlled bias in favour of the smaller interest categories.

Having worked out the desirable size of interest categories, the McClellan system then evolves a way of monitoring the stock within them. A series of record cards are produced which reveal at a glance the condition and effectiveness of the stock in each interest category, and an 'annual replacement target' is worked out which serves for the selector as the target figure of acquisitions for his category during the year. The calculations used to produce the replacement figure take into account three different types of *depreciation* affecting the stock:

1. depreciation through physical wear and tear of the books;
2. exhaustion of the stock by its readers (i.e. irrespective of its intrinsic value the stock no longer has enough 'unread' material to maintain an individual reader's interests);
3. obsolescence of the stock, as individual titles become less useful (progressively out-of-date, etc.) in the course of time.

Two other logistic problems are discussed by McClellan. In small interest categories the choice of stock offered to users at any one service point is bound to be restricted – despite the bias introduced by the square root formula. For the group of readers interested in that subject a state of stock exhaustion tends to be reached very quickly. If the stock in these categories is to be revised and replenished often enough at each service point to keep its readers supplied with fresh material, then buying of new titles will be at an extremely wasteful level – since few of the titles withdrawn would be out-of-date or physically obsolete at the time of their withdrawal. The best solution to this problem is the *exchange* of stock between different service points in the same authority.

The principle of exchange is urged as an essential component of the system. As an alternative to direct exchange between service points some authorities create circulating collections of 'low-interest' subjects which move location periodically without being assigned permanently to any base. This may well be the most effective answer to the problem of low-interest categories, and it is perhaps surprising that so few library authorities operate circulating collections – even given the administrative problems involved. Houghton's work in this area[92] makes some valuable practical points for effective circulating collections.

1. The stock must be chosen with great care. Typically it will include non-fiction books with a small but enthusiastic readership.
2. In fixing frequency of circulation, acquisition costs of the book should be measured against the total administrative costs

(especially transport) of circulation – the latter not to exceed the former.

3. The stock of circulating collections should not be catalogued, since the task of changing catalogue locations each time books are circulated would reduce the cost-effectiveness of the exercise very sharply.

Returning to McClellan, he also touches on the problem of titles which are so popular that they are constantly in circulation and therefore rarely available on the shelves to constitute part of the choice available to readers. For these titles librarians must link the 'rate of issue' factor to their own bibliographical knowledge to determine the rate of *duplication*. The issues of a book during the first year after its publication are likely to be influenced artificially by publicity, so that duplication during this period should be exercised as sparingly as possible.

We have seen how McClellan's system provides a framework for building up the bookstock at each service point. A target figure is reached for the total stock within each interest category, and the annual replacement figure is calculated from this and from examining the range of depreciation factors at work on the stock. The last and equally important part of the system concerns the *revision* of stock, in which all the factors bearing upon the stock which might cause it to depart from the logistic guidelines are carefully monitored and – where necessary – corrected. This provides in particular a double check that the actual shelf stock of any category does not exceed or fall short of the desired shelf stock. The revision phase of the operation differs from the initial phase in that it takes account of weaknesses (and strengths) inherent in the stock from previous years' book buying, and also in that it provides indications of the need for *weeding* the stock of individual categories, in addition to purchasing. The information collated for stock revision purposes includes a record of the age of the stock, together with indications of the obsolescence level and the reader exhaustion level described above.

All of this information, as it relates to each interest category, is recorded on another card – the stock record card – from which the condition of the stock in each category may be quickly evaluated. Priorities for revision between the interest categories may be determined by a comparison of the stock record cards.

The interpretation of information recorded on these cards is a complex process, to which McClellan devotes a chapter in *The logistics of public library bookstock.*[276]

This brief summary of the McClellan system has indicated the main factors involved in stock logistics, and the types of problems to be overcome. A shorthand presentation of this kind cannot convey all the modifying factors built into the system to add sophistication to the basic concept, nor the mathematical formulae used for working out the stock requirements. A reading of McClellan's own works on stock control is essential if the reader is to gain a balanced view of the system.

It is important to recognize that the McClellan system does not tell the selector which titles to buy. For this purpose bibliographical knowledge is required. What the system does do is to provide a continuous flow of information to the selector about the type of books required by the library and the number of books of each type, and it is on this information that the bibliographical decisions are based. McClellan has always been careful to stress that use of the stock control system must be counterbalanced by other aspects of the book provision process.

> . . . a too rigid adherence to the indications of the stock control system can be disadvantageous. Interpretations must be qualified by bibliographical knowledge, a real understanding of readers and reading and of the other 'feedback' systems within the organisation. Physical examination of the books on the shelves is a valuable corrective to misinterpretations of the records. The system is essentially diagnostic, the remedies are for the librarian to apply.[57]

McClellan carried out his original experiments in logistics during the period 1950 – 65, but the results were not encapsulated in book form until the appearance of *The logistics of a public library bookstock*[94] in 1978. The most recent substantial piece of work on public library stock logistics is described in Tony Houghton's *Bookstock management in public libraries* (1985),[92] again work based upon actual research carried out in a public library system. Curiously, Houghton makes no reference to McClellan, although his work covers much the same ground.

The reader may wish to make a choice between the two books – neither easy to read. Comparison is difficult, but McClellan's approach still seems the more deeply considered, and at the same time the more straightforward. Houghton places greatest stress upon achieving the maximum number of issues per book added to stock, rather than on achieving subject coverage on the shelves. His statement – 'A lending library after all is only a means of delivering a commodity to consumers in pretty much the same sort of way as a supermarket. So it should be governed by the same economic laws of supply and demand' – whilst in one sense salutary, may strike a chilling note to those who believe in the public library's responsibilities for satisfying minority tastes.

As McClellan constantly stresses, the interpretation of logistic information is crucial to its proper use. Houghton is a management analyst and appears to have only a hazy idea of how librarians organize book selection, and of the sources that they use. Moreover his approach is simplistic, treating each book as a vehicle for potential issues regardless of variations in type, level and style, and the differences in demand that these features suggest.

Another feature of Houghton's work is that he develops a very complex model for collecting logistic information, based upon sampling of the issue records of individual books in various categories – shelf stock, returned books, withdrawn books. Given that stock logistics cannot be an exact science and only provides an indication of use, McClellan's system of analysing loans and shelf stock statistics is simpler (particularly if issue statistics are analysed on a computer) and probably no less useful.

Nevertheless there is helpful new material in Houghton's book. His comments on the effects of injecting fresh stock into a subject area (Chapter 12) are illuminating, and his chapter (13) on bookstock rotation (exchanges) is very fully worked out and makes required reading.

Various criticisms have been made of McClellan's ideas, and some of these are reported in his chapter 'Critique and counter-critique'.[278] A common observation is that public library budgets of today do not permit many hours of staff time to be spent on the logistic aspects of stock control. Undoubtedly, application of the system does require generous staffing for book provision, and few public library authorities are currently able to contemplate additional staff posts on their establishments. However, as McClellan points out, this is a matter of priorities. Book provision is the foundation of good library service, and logistics are fundamental to good book provision. If these priorities are not reflected in the organization of staff the basis of the library service itself becomes progressively undermined.

Other criticisms of the McClellan system seem more valid. There are aspects of the scheme which appear either to distort information or to offer less sophisticated information than is required, and which would cause library authorities to examine its cost-effectiveness very closely before theory could be put into practice. These criticisms or limitations are noted below.

1. The interest categories themselves are fairly broad sub-divisions of the field of knowledge. To further subdivide them may make record-keeping impossibly complicated. Not to do so however is to run the risk of giving inappropriate treatment to different subjects within the same interest category. Minor subjects can easily be overlooked, and may not be represented in stock at all.

2. Within a subject the system allows little note to be taken of the level or function of material. This is a topic on which McClellan himself has written[279] and one which presents a fundamental problem to anyone planning book provision for public libraries.

3. Some of the measures used are crudely worked out. The square root formula is an entirely pragmatic solution to a difficult problem, as McClellan admits. The figures used to set the 'obsolescence rate' are arbitrary and take little account of subject differences.

4. It is hard to accept McClellan's assurance[280] that the system is responsive, to an extent, to 'unsatisfied demand'. The fact that unsatisfied demand is itself a complex and unresolved problem for librarians does not diminish the problem as it relates to stock logistics. Nor is it enough to point to other facets of the book provision system, such as the reservations service or staff relationships with readers, as a palliative. It is highly probable that many public library users do *not* make known unsatisfied demand, and any system which leans heavily on the use of existing stock as a barometer (as McClellan's does) is bound to be sensitive to this criticism.

Constructive criticism of McClellan's system is difficult since so few librarians have any practical experience of its application. At the present time most public library stock is chosen without any clear idea of the underlying stock needs of the user. A change in this situation can only be brought about by a change in attitude throughout the profession. Librarians needs to examine McClellan's proposals closely, evaluate the sophistication and accuracy of the information they produce, and offset these factors against cost. In one respect the outlook is encouraging. The detailed and time-consuming clerical procedures needed to record issues, sizes of stock categories and other stock data can obviously be undertaken more cost-effectively by computers.

These advances in automation, together with economies forced upon libraries by diminishing bookfunds, have generated some encouraging developments in the applications of logistic theories to public library bookstocks. Moore's article[95] describes the progress made in a handful of progressive authorities. Betts and Hargrave[90] give a detailed account of what has been achieved in one county. Although these activities only relate to a fraction of the total number of UK library authorities, it may be hoped that they foreshadow a revival of interest in an essential and much neglected component of the book provision process.

Academic and special libraries

McClellan's work on logistics relates to public library provision, where the wide subject range of user needs and the variety of levels of need render some form of logistic approach highly desirable. The fact that in practice logistic problems in public libraries are not given enough attention is noted above. In general, even less attention is paid to this aspect of provision in academic and special libraries. There are some valid reasons for this, principally the fact that the more limited range of user needs reduces the complexity of the operation of provision. Also, decisions on the purchase of multiple copies are rarely required in the case of research material. Nonetheless, logistics problems of making books available in special and academic libraries remain, and warrant research. Some studies have been made on the timing of decisions to relegate material to remote storage in universities (see Chapter 11) and on the relation between purchase and borrowing through interloans schemes (see Chapter 13).

Another area which warrants attention is that of short loan collections in universities. In his work *Book availability and the library users*,[91] Buckland reports on a study carried out on the short loan collection at Lancaster University, in which he relates both the loan period and the library's duplication policy to demand for individual titles. (With the short loan period reduced to one week, Lancaster found that the 11% of the monograph stock categorized as 'short loan' material generated as much as 47% of the open shelf borrowing.)

In addition to giving detailed reports of several research studies, Buckland's book also contains the best survey of the literature of stock logistics in academic and special libraries.

11 *Weeding*

Some definitions are needed. The term 'weeding' describes the removal of stock from library shelves, either for withdrawal, or for moving to reserve stock or to remote storage. 'Reserve stock' describes a closed access part of a library located in or near the same building as the open access collections. 'Remote storage' describes a closed access building located some distance from the main library.

'Withdrawal' means removal from the library stock either to be thrown away (discarding) or donated to another library. The moving of books to reserve stock or to remote storage is usually referred to as 'relegation'.

Sorting through stock on library shelves usually involves a number of other activities not strictly described by the term 'weeding' – for instance, identifying books for binding, replacement, cleaning, etc. These processes are described more fully in the chapter of this book on 'stock revision'.

There are two main reasons for weeding. The most basic is simply to clear space on the shelves to make room for new additions to stock. The second common motivation is the desire to increase the *use* of the stock – either by improving its appearance, so as to attract more users to the library, and/or by providing easier access to elements of the stock which are worthwhile, by removing the dead wood. The 'use' motivation is more common in public libraries, where the principle of providing an up-to-date stock of attractive appearance is more important, and where weeding is more commonly practised than in academic libraries. Also, the rate of use in public libraries is generally higher, so that physical delapidation of stock is more likely to set in, and oblige staff to weed. The matter of weeding policy in academic libraries as related to policy on collection size is discussed at greater length in Chapter 3.

Although it is likely that weeding does (if properly carried out) usually increase use of stock, the point is often a hard one to prove, since so many other factors bear upon stock use. One recent study by Williams[112] described the weeding of 20,000 volumes from a college of higher education, which did apparently result in a substantial rise in issues.

Materials are sent to reserve stock or remote storage because the open access shelf space is full, and/or because the use of closed access space is a cheaper option than extending the service areas of the library. Remote storage, with rudimentary heating, lighting and shelving, permits a considerable reduction in the costs of housing stock, whilst sacrificing the facility of immediate access.

Plausible reasons can usually be found for avoiding weeding. It is a laborious process, likely to lead to embarrassing blunders if badly done. The possibility that books may be needed at some future date tends to encourage a defensive strategy of retention. Moreover library procedures are generally designed to facilitate the addition of books, rather than their withdrawal. A further point in university libraries is that storage costs, though real enough, are not charged to the librarian's budget. Buckland[97] discusses in more detail some of these reasons for not weeding.

Some fundamental subjects relating to weeding are now explored in more detail. Firstly, weeding policy in any library is generally influenced by three background factors. These are: the cost of the weeding and the staff time needed to do it; the amount of open shelf space available; the size and effectiveness of the interloans services to which the library has access.

Secondly, the weeding process itself is usually based upon three criteria, described in more detail below. These are: non-use of stock, out-of-dateness of stock, and physical delapidation of stock.

Background to weeding policy

The cost of weeding

Despite incurring very real expenses, especially in the use of staff time, the costs of weeding are rarely built into the library budget. This is one reason why libraries do not always weed as much as they need to. Of course the retention of material on library shelves also costs money, in a sense, although a librarian may argue that it costs nothing extra to fill up shelf space which is lying empty. The real controversy arises when shelf space becomes full (see below).

In practice, university librarians have tended to identify the types of material which are *cheapest* to relegate, especially those whose location can be moved without major alterations to the catalogue records. This is, unashamedly, a policy of relegating by expediency rather than by any stated objectives. So, for instance, Taylor and Urquhart found[108] that the cost of relegating periodicals was about 13 times cheaper than for monographs. Ford comments[99] that other early candidates for relegation are special collections, books published before a certain date, or material in certain formats, e.g. pamphlets. In all these cases catalogues can be amended simply by a general notice explaining that the groups of materials have been moved to remote storage. Gilder's literature survey[101] contains a useful summary of information on the costs of relegation and various types of storage.

The amount of shelf space available

Secondly, and for obvious reasons, the size of a library's weeding programme is often determined by the amount of shelf space available. Whatever the desirable size of a library's stock, the practical starting point for this kind of decision must be the size of the library building itself, and other factors are subordinated to it except on the rare occasions that new libraries are planned. A librarian whose shelves are full is therefore obliged to weed at a rate which is precisely equal to that of his new accessions. This may often be undesirable, but it is a fact of life.

There is always, in theory at least, the option of a new and larger library building, although the chances of realizing this particular solution to full shelves are usually in the hands of luck and of various political factors. In the university field it was this problem which generated the appearance of the Atkinson Report[110] (see pp.9 – 10), itself a political solution. Brown[96] has made an interesting attempt to approach the situation from a more scientific basis. He estimates it is 'cheaper to discard books already in stock, rather than building additional storage space of reader access quality, if the books in question have a prospective frequency of use that has fallen below once in about 13 years'. Cost comparisons between retention and interlending are also relevant here. Nevertheless it should again be stressed that decisions about weeding programmes and/or new building programmes are rarely made on the basis of such calculations.

Effective interlending back-up

The importance of striking a balance between buying and borrowing is examined in Chapter 13, and in this respect the weeding of stock is also conditioned by the availability of other resources in the area. Librarians will be aware of the various interlending schemes available to them, their coverage and effectiveness, and the type of material which can and cannot be borrowed. Stock which is withdrawn should be offered to other libraries participating in the interlending network. It is also sensible to try and find out the likelihood of offers being accepted. Ford's survey[99] of a sample of relegated stock from two university libraries showed that 75% of the relegated stock was not held by BLLD, notably foreign language and pre-1900 material.

Criteria for weeding

McClellan's work on stock logistics in public libraries[94] suggests formulae which indicate to the librarian *when* sections of the stock need revision. A separate problem, examined in the following pages, is how to decide *which* titles should be withdrawn from any one section of the stock.

More often than not the principal criterion used in practice for weeding of all types of collections is the subjective one of 'the librarian's own judgement', based upon a knowledge of the users and of the subject literatures covered by the collection. In a public or university library which does not have subject specialists on its staff – or even in those that do – this places an intolerably heavy burden of responsibility on the individual's judgement, and it is unlikely that any one person called upon to make weeding decisions over a spectrum of subject fields will on the basis of judgement alone achieve a consistent rate of 'correct' decision making. With more than one person engaged in weeding the possibility of consistency is further diminished. Judgement can never be excluded from the weeding process, but in recent years practitioners and researchers have sought a more reliable weeding criterion which can be applied scientifically to produce consistent results.

A basic assumption of the weeding process is that the value of a book to the members of a particular library can be estimated from the *use* made of it. The relegation of less frequently used books to remote storage should eventually increase the overall relevance of the stock to users' needs and therefore lead to a more efficient use of resources (assuming that books which replace the neglected material issue more frequently).

Much of the controversy in the literature of weeding is over the most effective method of predicting the future use of a collection. One school of thought affirms that *use of the existing collection* is the best predictor. Other writers feel that the *imprint date* of items in the collection is just as accurate a predictor, and easier to apply. Hart's *Book selection and use in academic libraries*[102] provides a useful summary of recent literature.

Fussler and Simon, in *Patterns in the use of books in large research libraries*,[100] affirmed that 'past use over a sufficiently long period is an excellent and by far the best predictor of future use', although they observed, 'the confidence limits of prediction vary significantly from one subject to another'. Trueswell[109] and Slote[107] are also exponents of the 'past use' theory. Their work on library weeding begins from the premise that the open access areas of the library should house the *core collection* – which is defined by Slote as the materials 'most likely to be used by the clients', and that the core collection can be predicted accurately from a study of use of the existing collection. Using the Slote method the librarian retains a collection which satisfies a predetermined amount of future use – so that, for instance, he tries to identify the 'core' which would satisfy 95% (or 99%) of the present demands made upon the collection.

Slote's method of predicting future use from past use is based upon analysis of the 'shelf time period' – i.e. the length of time a book remains upon the shelf between successive uses. He claims that the last shelf time period recorded on a book is highly predictive of future use, and gives a description of a simple method by which such information is examined and analysed to provide a basis for the weeding of stock. He also notes alternative methods for libraries which do not record issues on date labels in the books, and he shows how to predict the number of books which will be weeded at a given level of future use.

An important criticism of Slote's and Trueswell's theories is put forward by Taylor and Urquhart in their research study *Management and assessment of stock control in academic libraries*[108] in which they claim that the main predictor of future use in a research collection is not the frequency of past use but the *imprint date* of items in the collection. Taylor and Urquhart observe that, for the great majority of research materials, use of an item declines rapidly about three years after publication, so that after this period any book has an equally low chance of being used. They have some fairly disparaging comments to make about the study of 'use' as a predictor for weeding.

> Monograph relegation based on date labels is highly suspect. If it is known that a group of books is little used then the borrowing record of items from that group is a nil predictor of future use ... unfortunately the satisfying ritual of checking date labels gives the illusion that all is well and seems to be scientifically ennobled. The relegating acolyte does not realise that after a certain date nearly every book is as good or as bad a case as another.

The criticism of the 'past use' method makes a valid point, but the substitution of imprint date as the criterion for weeding begs some questions. Without doubt weeding of research collections by imprint date is cheaper to carry out than weeding by past circulation – a point established, for scientific materials at least, by Raffell and Shishko in *Systematic analysis of university libraries.*[105] It cannot, however, be claimed with any certainty that it is a more *accurate* method. In general terms the use of research material in libraries is known to decline with age, but the rate of decline within different disciplines shows considerable variation. Additionally, there are works in every subject field which resist the 'standard' rate of decline for their subjects. Taylor and Urquhart concede that such works may comprise as much as 10% of the total and suggest that when the date of imprint method is used for weeding the 10% must be identified in some other way. No other way is suggested, however. Their recommendation is to relegate arbitrarily once books are no longer new. A margin of error of 10% is seen as acceptable.

In practice it is possible to combine the two methods. Salford University, for instance, relegate on the basis of two features: a cut-off date of 1930, and a measure of the number of uses in the previous five years.

Some writers have attempted to draw up some general guidelines which relate the weeding of research material to the concept of *obsolescence* – the diminution in the use of literature over the course of time. The subject of obsolescence has generated a considerable amount of literature, most of it based on citation studies – that is, studies showing the number of times that individual books or periodical articles are cited in the lists of references given at the end of a piece of research (a method, it can be seen, which is distinct from studies of actual library use). It is known that all forms of research literature do obsolesce, and that there are considerable differences between the pattern of obsolescence of different subject areas. If it were possible to draw up reasonably accurate guidelines showing the rate of decline in use for each subject this would clearly serve as valuable background information for the librarian attempting to make discard or relegation decisions on individual volumes within those subject areas.

An extensive survey of obsolescence studies by Line and Sandison,[104] however, concludes that the librarian can make little practical use of the concept of obsolescence. The authors observe that up to the present time most obsolescence studies have been characterized by a superficial approach to what is a highly complex situation of interlocking factors. The relationship between citation and use is particularly complicated, and it is not yet known what factors determine which items in a collection will be read or cited and the relative importance of age among them. Line and Sandison conclude, 'Variations between individual titles, of serials as well as monographs, are likely to be so great that substantial data must be collected for each individual title, perhaps in each library (certainly in each type of library) if weeding is to be done on a rational basis'.

It may be seen from the above that the controversy between 'past use' and imprint date as a criterion for weeding has still to be resolved. A further criticism may be levelled against the 'past use' theory of weeding, particularly when it is applied to public libraries, where most of Slote's studies were carried out. The criticism relates to the proposal that a single standard can be used to determine weeding for large sections of stock. Slote concedes that in determining how much of a stock should be retained, separate percentages may have to be fixed for different sections of the stock, such as fiction and non-fiction. One would however have to go much further than this. In fact, it is difficult to envisage any library which would not require a considerable number of categories to take account of varying rates of use for different subjects and levels of requirement. This applies particularly to public libraries, which aim to satisfy a wide range of reading needs at a number of different levels. The need for varying criteria extends even to fiction stock, in which field most of Slote's own studies were carried out. No public librarian, for instance, can regard each item on the fiction shelves as an equal unit, to be discarded if its rate of use falls below the average rate for the entire stock. Different rates of use are expected of 'serious' and 'recreational' fiction – and within these groupings certain types of works (e.g. Bulgarian novels in translation) must be expected to issue less frequently than others (e.g. novels by Graham Greene).

It is clear that if a method of examining use is to be devised which does not lean entirely upon the librarian's judgement, that method must be sophisticated enough to take into account the many variable factors. McClellan goes some way towards achieving this with his 'mean issue per book ratio'.[281] Taking each of his subject categories in turn he divides the total annual issues by the number of books in the category to achieve a nominal figure of the average number of issues per book. The performance of any individual title in the category can thus be assessed by comparing the issue record on its date label with the 'mean issue per book ratio'.

No firm recommendations on weeding practice can be drawn from the conflicting findings of these reports. Until more conclusive evidence is available librarians will probably continue to use their own judgements in a particular local situation, allied to general guidelines formulated from a study of both use and date of publication.

One further point should be made in relation to use as an indicator. Neither issue statistics nor the study of date labels in the books record in-house use, which may often be substantial. Fussler and Simon,[100] and others, have found loan use to be a reasonably good predictor of in-house use, but the subject is a highly complex one. It is explored in more detail on pp.36 – 7.

Two other valid criteria for weeding may be employed in conjunction with use and publication date. The physical condition of stock is a matter of some importance, especially in public libraries, school libraries and any other collections for which an element of book promotion is appropriate. Libraries of this kind normally aim to achieve a certain standard of appearance in their bookstock, though the standard itself is inevitably governed by the size of the bookfund. The situation may be contrasted with that in a university library where users are more highly motivated and the presentation of stock is not an important factor.

Relating individual books to an acceptable physical standard is very much a subjective matter, though certain minimum standards should apply in most situations – e.g. pages which are not badly stained, bindings on which the words of the title can be deciphered. A good deal can be achieved inexpensively through repair (for instance of torn or loose pages) or through the simple expedient of cleaning laminated covers.

Books may also be withdrawn if their content becomes out-of-date *even though* they are still being used. The implication of this is that in some kinds of library the librarian acknowledges a degree of responsibility to his users, who may not themselves know whether a particular item contains reliable information. An obvious example is that old editions are normally withdrawn from library shelves as new editions are added to stock. Equally, the content of one book may be superseded by another entirely different work containing new facts or a more modern approach.

But whether it is superseded by a new work or not, any book of a popular or educational nature which is clearly out of date should be considered for discard. For a librarian to 'screen' stock in this way is usually seen as standard library procedure in a library for children, but is less often accepted in relation to adult reading. Nevertheless there is a clear case for its practice in public libraries, and even in university provision for undergraduates. It is generally assumed that at postgraduate level and above users can look after themselves.

One other factor influences weeding policy, as it does selection policy. In many libraries there is some tension between what users want (or say they want, or think they want) and what the librarian feels they need. This is seen most clearly in libraries whose function is educational (in the broadest sense). A librarian may build up sections of the stock that he feels are important even though there is no immediate response in terms of issues. Alternatively, he may insist that certain important works are retained in stock, whether used or not. For such a policy to be effective the librarian should ensure that works selected or retained on this basis are accorded additional promotion in the library. Should this still fail to stimulate use it may be practical to recognize an error in selection, and discard accordingly.

Binding

Publishers' casings are not designed for library use, and if subjected to a heavy rate of issues they may become damaged within a year or two of purchase. The librarian is then confronted with a decision which is almost as important (and almost as costly) as his original selection decision. He may choose to have the book bound, but this is by no means an automatic decision. The 'bound' book suffers from some major disadvantages if placed in competition with its unbound counterpart. In the first place, its content is less up-to-date than a more recent book on the same subject. Secondly, its appearance is less attractive than an unbound book, which carries the original dust jacket intact (though there are still a handful of traditionalists or binding fetishists who prefer the appearance of a library binding to a laminated dust jacket).

Many public librarians therefore prefer to discard a damaged book and replace it with a new copy of the same title or with another book altogether. In a small collection the latter option affords the advantage of giving greater variety to the stock. The cost of replacement should be compared with the cost of binding as another factor influencing a decision. As a general rule books intended to attract 'browsing' readers are much less likely to warrant binding. Binding is most appropriate for books which are specifically sought, by author or title, irrespective of their appearance. Standard works required for long-term retention on open access stock would obviously be bound – though works intended for relegation to store need not be unless their physical condition impedes use.

Most library suppliers produce 'library editions' of fiction by buying up sets of book sheets from the publishers, adding double strength reinforcing and laminating the dust jackets on to their own boards – the end result having far greater durability than a publisher's casing, and avoiding the need for binding after a couple of years' use.

For the librarian from a research library, different factors apply. There is no need to attract readers by displaying books in good condition – so that this motivation to bind is removed. On the other hand most research materials are retained in stock indefinitely, so that for any work where the condition has seriously deteriorated the tendency is to bind rather than to discard.

The type of binding chosen for any individual volume must always be related to the type and size of the book and its estimated length of retention. Kirby[103] gives a useful run-down of available styles.

Part II

Background

12 *Management*

Management is a pervasive activity, and material on the management of book provision is scattered throughout this book. For instance, the preceding chapters on 'policy' and on 'budgeting' are fundamental to discussion of management issues. The purpose of the present chapter is to note some of the practical difficulties of managing book provision programmes, to try and suggest minimum system requirements for effective management and finally to outline briefly the important features of existing management systems.

The literature of library management is disappointing, comprising, for the most part, examples from library operations tacked onto a reiteration of general management principles. There are few examinations of the special management problems thrown up by library systems, and the area could provide a fruitful one for future work.

Management problems in book provision

Book provision generates some particularly intractable management problems, especially in the area of quality control of work carried out. These are noted below, together with possible approaches to solutions. One difficulty is the lack of formal education in book provision methods, which especially affects librarians in their first or second posts. A survey by Roberts and Bull[300] of postgraduate library students' first posts showed that book selection and acquisition was a prominent duty for many of them; the first four duties reported were cataloguing and classification (94% of the sample of students), reference and readers' advisory work (76%), selection and acquisition (67%) and management (38%). It is likely that someone taking up a post direct from library school will have far less practical or quasi-practical experience of book selection than of the two preceding activities, and this may mean that the manager needs to introduce his staff to the basic elements of book provision work in addition to the special features of a particular system. These problems point very clearly to the need for training, and many library systems would benefit from the introduction of regular training courses (of up to a week in duration) on book provision. Some library authorities already hold such courses.

Motivation of staff can also be a problem, since the results of good book provision are less clearly visible than, say, the results of effective information work (where an enquirer is likely to make satisfaction immediately known to the staff concerned). The effects of book selection, on the other hand, only filter through months or years after the work has been carried out, to be partially detected, if at all, in issue statistics or chance comments from users. Probably the only person really aware of how good a job has been done is the selector and the selector's line manager. The need for close supervision is therefore apparent, although this in itself presents problems.

The difficulties of supervision stem largely from the detailed nature of book provision work. In any one day's activity a selector makes a large number of separate decisions about particular titles, each decision reflecting a range of background circumstances, some of them quite complex. To be sure of maintaining quality control over this, a manager would need to cover much of the same ground personally, something clearly out of the question. Instead he or she must hope to get by with a combination of other measures – a clear and detailed policy statement, training, frequent discussions on practice and spot checks of work completed. One problem about statements of policy or principle is that they often need (in the nature of things) to refer to generalized concepts of types or levels of books – e.g. an undergraduate text – whereas in practice such definitions are notoriously difficult to apply to particular works (see pp.42 – 3).

The important contribution made to book provision by the personal flair of the selector creates further difficulties for the manager, and requires him or her to exercise fine judgement and sensitivity in supervising the work of members of the team. This factor should not be over-emphasized, since most book provision systems could be more scientifically managed than they are, but nor should it be dismissed.

The problems noted above are intensified for the management of stock revision programmes; these are carried out by staff who are either subject specialists or who have in the course of the stock revision acquired a good deal of knowledge about the subject literature – certainly more than the line manager. Nonetheless, some form of control needs to be devised. Checks on weeded volumes or on the physical quality of stock left on the shelves are reasonably easy to apply. The overall expenditure on any one subject must be regulated, taking into account use and objectives and relating these to other subjects. The choice of bibliographies used can be monitored and spot checks made on the orders proposed, taking some limited subject areas and using sections of a reliable and up-to-date bibliography.

Finally worth mentioning are the complex logistics of the raw materials of book provision themselves. Selectors deal with material which becomes available and unavailable on an irregular and increasingly unpredictable basis. They must consider all new books as well as the old ones, and must therefore hold back enough funds to cover those books which appear at the end of the financial year. They must not underspend or overspend, and must regularize the volume of books received so that the processing departments have an even flow of work throughout the year. All this calls for a very careful and flexible system of budgeting and control, particularly at the outset and during the last three months of the year.

Minimum system requirements
The most important factor is for the library system as a whole to be organized so as to achieve its primary purpose: that is, the provision of books and other materials, leading to the provision of information. An article by McClellan, 'A systems approach to libraries'[116] provides a useful model, suggesting that 'library objectives' *take effect in* 'book provision policies and book provision organisation', and distinguishing these from the secondary 'organisation systems' that are necessary for the achievement of primary objectives.

Different types of library have different needs, and it is not therefore possible to suggest any one system as a model. However, the following proposals are tentatively put forward as minimum requirements for most kinds of library.

1. A detailed book provision policy exists and is made known to all members of staff. Codes of practice are also made available, detailing criteria for selection and methods to be used.

2. Policy is implemented by earmarking specific sums for specific purposes and by monitoring orders to ensure that these financial guidelines are adhered to.

3. Further financial guidelines are required to ensure that a throughout-the-year coverage of new publications is guaranteed, and that orders (and therefore the receipt of books) are evenly paced throughout the year.

4. Book provision in any one system is centrally coordinated – though in very large systems a regional or subsystem structure may take over many of the coordination functions. A balance is struck between the stated needs of staff from individual service points and the needs of the system or subsystem. The need for coordination of activity applies to all features of book provision, including stock revision and weeding. Where feasible, activity in one part of the system should be so organized as to have an effect in other parts (for instance, the results of stock revision at one service point can be used in all others). The vital function of ensuring overall coverage of new publications must be centrally organized.

5. The selection of newly published books is linked to a single base source of information (see Chapter 8) and wherever possible decisions are reached through a pooling of knowledge by staff.

6. A specified minimum proportion of total staff work hours is devoted to book provision. A specified amount appears to be necessary because of a common tendency to cut down on book provision work whenever there is pressure on staff time. In public libraries, sufficient expenditure of staff time and money is given to the activity of stock revision (see p.66).

7. A regular programme of staff training for book provision is introduced.

8. Detailed statistical information about book orders, stock, and its use, is maintained in a way that throws light on the achievement (or non-achievement) of library objectives. Such information is regularly scanned by management.

Existing systems

Public libraries

Before the reorganization of British local government in 1972 book selection in many of the smaller borough authorities was virtually operated on a personal basis by the librarian and/or his deputy. Although some excellent bookstocks were built up in this manner, the disadvantages of such a system are clear. One person can scarcely have the time or the expertise needed to find out what has been published and link this to readers' needs throughout his authority, especially when book provision is only one of his many responsibilities.

The converse of the one-man system – used in some of the old county libraries, and still to be found in some authorities today – is for librarians at service points to be given virtually complete control of selection for their own stock. The bookfund is divided into separate allocations for each service point and little or no control is exercised over the way these amounts are spent. Again, the disadvantages are plain enough. The system leads to over-duplication of popular titles, neglect of more expensive and serious works, duplication of effort and waste of money.

From the 1950s onwards authorities began to create specialist posts, usually called 'stock editors', to work full time on book provision. The stock editor generally concentrated on stock revision and supervision of withdrawals, but in some authorities he or she also played a large part in the selection of new books. He or she might also be responsible for a large department providing the bibliographical services of cataloguing, reservations and interloans. The theory behind the stock editor approach was that one person (or group of people) working full time on the bookstock could achieve a more penetrating and unified approach, and that the stock editor could pay more detailed attention to such matters as checks on withdrawals, coverage of specialist reviews, and the perusal of lists of secondhand books. The stock editor system reached a point in some authorities where work on the stock was turned over almost entirely to the 'specialist' officer, and librarians at service points were denied any real voice in stock provision.

None of these methods of book provision are suitable for the British public library authorities created by the 1972 reorganization of local government, in which bookstocks have to serve a large number of service points (usually more than 20, sometimes as many as 70) scattered over a very large area. As one would expect, the organization of book provision within the new authorities shows a wide variety of approaches. Nevertheless, a basic pattern emerges. Responsibility for bibliographical services over the whole authority normally resides with a senior officer based at headquarters – a post usually known as Bibliographical Services Officer, less commonly as Stock Editor. This officer administers a large department which provides the centralized services of cataloguing, interloans, reservations and book processing. Sometimes there are also specialist staff in the department responsible for book selection and stock revision.

A bibliographical services officer has three main duties. He has to formulate and promote book provision policy in the authority. He must see that policy is put into practice. And he administers the service departments. Most of the actual work of book provision is operated on an *area* basis – in common with other functions of the library service. Some authorities have area stock editors, responsible for coordinating provision in their area. More often, coordination of book provision is the responsibility of the area librarian, working through some or all of his professional staff. Sometimes staff are organized into 'professional service teams', either split up on a subject specialization basis, or – more usually – attached to service points in the traditional manner. The function of the areas is to achieve more or less complete coverage of popular and standard works for their zone. The bibliographical services officer subsequently ensures that more specialized works not ordered by the areas are at some point put into the stock of the authority as a whole.

A recent survey *Trends in public library selection policies*[13] suggests that most selection decisions are taken by district or branch librarians, with a 15 – 20% in-fill from the head of bibliographical services post in authorities which have a form of central selection (not all do).

The main variation on the area theme tends to occur in authorities which are based on a very large city collection. In such cases, the 'reference' collections of the city library are normally divided up into subject departments, each of these more or less autonomous in its selection of materials. It is assumed that overall coverage of new publications in the authority is achieved by these departments. Service points outside the 'central' library are grouped together on the familiar area basis. There is rarely any real contact between areas and reference departments in the matter of book provision.

A kind of 'halfway house' between the area system and the reference departments/area system has been reached by some of the authorities which do not have a large city collection within their boundaries, but feel that the needs of the 'serious' reader should nevertheless be given special attention. In these authorities the function of 'filling in' important works not ordered by the areas is given to a central resources unit, a team of professional librarians headed by the bibliographical services officer, with authority-wide responsibility for selecting published works of any importance. The team usually comprises a number of subject specialists who either build up major collections in their specializations (often, but not necessarily located at the central library) or allocate titles to appropriate service points throughout the authority.

The usual method for reconciling different shades of opinion within the authority (or area) is the *book meeting*, at which representatives of the bibliographical services department and/or the areas meet on a regular basis to discuss the selection of new books.

It must be said that in Britain the new public library authorities created in 1972 have in many cases failed to capitalize on the opportunities for better stock provision which the larger units were supposedly able to achieve. Implementation of policy (where one exists) lacks conviction. There is often a lack of real coordination between area or central authorities and individual service points. The vital function of ensuring coverage of new publications is haphazard. Finally, the amount of staff time devoted to book provision frequently falls sadly below what is necessary.

University libraries
In university libraries the organization of staff for book provision has to resolve a major difficulty – the respective roles of university departments *vis-à-vis* the library staff. In practice, systems may be found which favour either party. Some university administrations give almost total control of the bookfund to the librarian, with suggestions from departments and faculties permitted, but

not particularly encouraged. Others divide up the bookfund on a departmental basis and leave the librarian only a minimal allocation to balance up departmental orders.

Neither of these extreme solutions is satisfactory. Not to make full use of the subject expertise of the university lecturing and research staff for selection is obviously absurd. At the same time, a system which relies entirely upon departmental selection is bound to result in lack of balance. Some lecturers are more enthusiastic than others in building up library collections in their subjects. Some are more knowledgeable than others about their subject literatures. However effective the departmental ordering, some central control is needed to balance up inequality of treatment between subjects, order interdisciplinary material, and fill in titles which for one reason or another have been missed.

Most universities now opt for a system which combines the best features of both approaches. The librarian normally retains control of the ordering process, and sometimes has complete control over the bookfund. Alternatively, departments have an allocation, while the library retains a generous contingency fund. The librarian brings items to the attention of lecturers and gives advice where needed. Suggestions from departments are automatically ordered (unless funds have run out).

Evans[259] suggests – in one academic library study – that books selected by librarians circulate more freely than those selected by academic staff. This may be the case in some circumstances, but there is no evidence available to suggest that it is generally true.

In his report *Developing an acquisitions system for a university library*,[115] Hindle proposes a system in which university departments are responsible for the development of research collections, while library staff control the provision of teaching materials.

Whenever the library does play the controlling role in the book selection process there must be one person within the library with overall responsibility for that function. The librarian himself may well be closely involved, but the controlling function normally rests with head of acquisitions. He/she in turn coordinates the work of other staff involved – the subject specialist librarians (see next section) and/or the departmental representatives appointed to coordinate their department's requirements with the library staff. Whatever the precise arrangement, a strong liaison maintained between library staff and individual departments is essential. In the background, beyond the executive structure, will be the library committee – to which any particular problems may be put. For instance, some librarians consult their committee (or a subcommittee of it) about new periodical titles, often a controversial matter since it cuts across a number of different subject fields. The way that these arrangements for the responsibility and control of book provision work out are often as much a matter of personalities and university politics as anything else. Norman Higham's book[114] contains a discussion of the various permutations possible, together with some advice from experience.

Where a university administers a number of special subject or departmental collections physically separate from the main library, the tendency to have separate departmental funding and separate responsibility for selection is usually more pronounced. Some universities have 50 or more departmental libraries of this kind. In this situation the need for an overall control of book provision needs to be carefully examined. Hindle's survey at the University of Lancaster, where a departmental selection system operated, showed that in one year a total of 17 departments had added books on the subject of 'operational research' to their collections – two of these ordering more titles than the operational research department itself.

Nevertheless in a very large institution such as the University of London, with large and geographically scattered subject collections, a divide and rule system is inevitable, and in contrast to Hindle's findings, a survey on the 'Overlap of acquisitions in the University of London Libraries'[118] found that duplication in this kind of situation was in fact relatively small. An examination of the catalogue entries for 20,000 *British national bibliography* titles ordered during one six-month period for 49 University of London libraries revealed no more than 1.85 entries per title – hardly disturbing evidence of duplicate ordering.

Subject specialization
Most university libraries in Britain have appointed to their staffs some subject specialists, with qualifications in a subject as well as in librarianship, to be responsible for book selection and

reference and information work (and sometimes other activities) within their specialization. A survey in 1982 of 61 British academic libraries by Woodhead and Martin[311] showed that 40 of the libraries used subject specialists in this way, to varying degrees. Such staff usually have a close relationship with the academic departments.

Despite the problems caused by multisite operations and the multidisciplinary nature of courses, most British polytechnics also use the subject librarian approach – see Higginbottom's paper.[113]

This arrangement, which appears to have much to recommend it in professional terms as well as adding to the attraction of professional posts for recruiting purposes, has not been taken up on any scale by public libraries. Some public library authorities do have subject specialist posts on their staffs, notably in the subject-based reference departments which exist in some of the large metropolitan libraries. Few, however, reflect the kind of commitment to effective professional service which inspired McClellan's system in the borough of Tottenham in the 1950s.

McClellan has written that 'the knowledge of books is so important a requirement in each factor of book provision that an organisation of staff based on bibliography seems self-evident'. The required staff structure is described in full in his paper 'The organisation of a library for subject specialisation'.[116] A brief summary of this article is given here.

The trend towards categorization of public library staff into specialist posts – cataloguers and classifiers, readers' advisers, stock editors, administrators – has had the result of cutting off most librarians from contact with their readers. Readers require from librarians a knowledge of user needs allied to a knowledge of books. In the Tottenham system, which is bibliographically based, administrative duties are separated from bibliographical duties and carried out by non-professional staff from an administrative division. The 'bibliographical division' is divided into subject groups, each of which is responsible for professional duties in one service point of the authority, and also for all the bibliographical responsibilities in the subject field allocated to it. These duties are listed as: the preparation of desiderata lists; the selection and purchase of books within broad terms of reference; allocation of books between libraries; classification and cataloguing of all books and materials; revision of stock; screening of withdrawn books; screening of books for rebinding; maintenance of central reserve stocks; bibliographical work, including compilation of special lists and indexes; the bibliographical aspects of inter-library loans and regional loans and of readers' requests and reservations; readers' advisory and information service.

McClellan feels that the advantages to the librarian of this arrangement are that he is able to exercise constantly all his professional skills and avoid being bogged down by a heavy burden of administrative routine. Any librarian involved in the selection of material is also constantly in touch with readers, so that an over-theoretical approach based merely upon the bibliographical and logistic aspects of provision is more likely to be avoided.

The advantages to the reader are that he 'turns for help to the professional staff; he learns to appreciate that his needs are not restricted by the limitations of the bookstock of one library. He learns also to appreciate the possibilities open to him from using the skills of the professional librarian versed in bibliography and at home in the world of books. The arrangement makes possible a more intensive personal service and at the same time stimulates it.'

There are some problems attached to the operation of the scheme. It requires a larger scale of staff resources than would normally be available, and in a climate of economic cut-backs this is a serious limitation. The subdivision of stock into subject groups calls for flexible and adroit administration. The whole system requires firm management and a continuous impetus from the top to ensure that the diffusion of staff duties does not result in diffusion of the work rate.

Evaluation of the McClellan system is difficult because there have been so few opportunities to see it in operation. McClellan's own authority, Tottenham Public Libraries, used it with success, and in the local government reorganization of Greater London, Haringey adopted the system from them. A few other authorities have taken over elements of the scheme. The separation of administrative and professional activities and the use of 'floating' groups of professional librarians within an authority has found some exponents, but the stress on attention to the stock, which was the key to McClellan's thinking, has not been followed up (although many universities now operate a subject specialist system). The 1970s were not characterized by an emphasis on the bibliographical aspects of librarianship, and the possibility of

107

wide-scale application of McClellan's ideas seem more remote now than it did 20 years ago. The ideas themselves are none the less valid despite this neglect.

13 *Interlending*

Discussion of budgeting and costs leads on to another important factor. To what extent can any library system, of any type, attempt to acquire all the publications which might be relevant to its purpose? In recent years there have been very large increases in the number of new publications appearing on the market. Britain alone published over 60,000 new titles and new editions in 1990. The number of published periodical titles continues to rise. Reports, theses and conference proceedings, amongst other materials, are increasingly being made accessible to libraries. If one looks at the international scene – as any university or special librarian must – the range of choice is further amplified, especially since publishing in the Third World is expanding very quickly. Furthermore, against the difficulties of selecting for new materials can be added those relating to a vast retrospective choice. Finally, the problem of quantity is made more obvious by improved bibliographical control, and more pressing by increases in the amount and diversity of demand from users.

It is generally accepted now that to speak of self-sufficiency in the face of such quantities of material is absurd. Yet, at the same time, the process of obtaining material through interlending schemes is expensive and time-consuming, and only to be undertaken for groups of material which are infrequently needed by the library's clientele, or which – because they are out-of-print – cannot be purchased for library stock. Crudely expressed, the librarian's aim must be to acquire for stock the materials which are likely to be most frequently used. In this he/she will be influenced by a knowledge of what is available in other institutions in the locality (and if cooperative arrangements for acquisition can be made, so much the better). He/she will also be aware of the possibilities for borrowing – both nationally and internationally.

The obvious question arises – what amount of use would justify material being purchased for library stock rather than borrowed through the interlending network? This cannot be precisely quantified, but several writers have had a stab at a formula. The stimulating article *Some library costs and options*[105] by Brown (an economist) concludes 'it seems to be worth acquiring and providing storage for, books likely to be wanted more often than once in about 1.7 years over a long period'. Line's paper[108] takes a slightly different approach, estimating (in 1983) the average cost of an inter-library borrowing to a requesting library in UK to be approximately £4, and the average price of a book to be £10 plus £7 or £8 for acquisition and processing, and therefore deducing it to be cheaper to make five borrowings of a title before purchase. Williams[253] made similar deductions following a study carried out in the United States.

All three writers are at pains to stress the unquantifiable advantages of purchase as against borrowing. In particular, purchase allows the possibility (which borrowing rules out) of in-house use of materials, which may be quite heavy (although Brown also comments that in some university libraries 70% of the stock has remained unused over a three-year period). These lines of discussion lead directly into the perpetual controversy over browsing, and whether it is useful or practical for research work.

From the user's point of view, the source of a requested item is of far less interest than speed of supply. Any reader seeking an individual document at a library will be offered one of three different levels of service:

1. immediate supply from stock;
2. supply from within the library system but not from the particular service point;
3. supply from an external location.

In this connection McClellan has written that the librarian does not reject books, but places them on a 'scale of accessibility'.[255] However, in terms of time and delays in supply this stratification of service usually results in being decreasingly satisfactory to the reader whose request falls into category 2 or 3. A mitigating circumstance is the fact that few library users restrict themselves to one source alone for obtaining books. Luckham's survey of public library use, for instance, notes that only 24% of users obtained all their needs from a single public library service point.[254]

There is also evidence to suggest that, in research work at least, delays in supply cause less concern than might be expected. A survey by Houghton and Prosser[266] found that delays were not a major problem for a research worker borrowing copies of periodical articles through the interlending system. This is perhaps just as well, since White's informative 1985 survey of interlending in the UK [124] found that the percentage of UK requests satisfied within a period of seven days (from all sources) had declined from 50% in 1977 to 32% in 1985.

For the purposes of simplification, library interlending may be seen as falling into one of two basic groups. In the first of these a group of libraries cooperate because of a factor or factors which they hold in common – usually their subject field or their geographical location. In the second, libraries draw upon the resources of one central or major collection. (Line outlines a more complex model than this in his article *Access to collections, including inter-library loans.* [122])

The first of these groups affords opportunities for cooperative acquisition in addition to interloans. For instance, the well-known Farmington Plan, which operated from 1948 to 1972, was a voluntary agreement between 60 American libraries to acquire at least one copy of each new foreign publication that might reasonably be expected to interest a research worker. Gwinn's 1982 article[120] describes the more recent 'Conspectus' scheme of the US Research Libraries Group, which has evolved a method for recording the selection policies and holdings of libraries, with a view to affecting collection development. The idea has been taken up by the British Library, and by Scottish university libraries, though no dramatic results appear to have been registered so far as acquisition practice is concerned.

Cooperative acquisition may be taken a stage further if a system of centralized acquisition is introduced. Probably the best example of this is the Mid-West Interlibrary Center (MILC) started in 1948 (now the Center for Research Libraries) in which a group of the major university libraries of the American Mid-west introduced a scheme for the sharing of little-used research items. The point (compared with cooperative acquisition) is that all the purchased items are centralized at a site on the University of

Chicago, rather than scattered amongst the participating libraries.

In Britain, the Regional Library Bureaux have consistently handled both interlending and cooperative acquisition programmes, although their share of the total national interlending activity is only 8% – largely derived from handling types of material which are not stocked by the British Library Document Supply Centre (BLDSC – see below). The Consortium of University Research Libraries (CURL) is a more recent initiative, involving the major British academic libraries, whose catalogue records are made available to each other, and (through the Joint Academic Network) to other UK university libraries. Heaney, in describing this development[265] feels that university interlending patterns *vis-à-vis* BLDSC might eventually be affected.

Some 11% of interlending in UK is 'direct' lending between two libraries – i.e. not passing through any formal network. There are also some examples of local cooperation between – for instance – public libraries and technical colleges in the same geographical area, many of these systems offering technical information services to local firms.

However, an important study, *Local library co-operation*[110] published in 1974 found that the scope for savings through cooperative acquisition locally was very small. The duplication of titles amongst the different types of institution studied in Sheffield was found to be very low, and in view of the fact that cooperative acquisition is not simple to introduce and that central purchasing agencies tend to delay orders, the authors recommended against it. They did however feel that it was worth coordinating the acquisition of reference material and the retention of periodical titles. In practice, cooperation in British libraries most often centres upon interloans, information services, shared cataloguing, and the mutual promotion of each other's resources.

The second main type of lending occurs when libraries borrow from one major centre, which because of the size of its collections can provide an effective service on a large scale. (This sometimes happens on a small scale, within a defined subject area. For instance, some British libraries take out institutional membership with *Law notes*, to give themselves access to a quick loan service for expensive textbooks in law. Similarly, institutional membership of the London Library affords access to a collection of rare works in literature and the humanities.)

Britain is virtually the only country with a major collection which gives a service of this kind for all subjects. The British Library Document Supply Centre (BLDSC) is by far the most comprehensive organization of its kind in the world, handling 72% of UK lending, as well as over half of all international interlending, and achieving a success rate of 92% on all requests. Any British libraries selecting for (or withdrawing from) their own stock need to be aware of the services offered by BLDSC, and of the strengths and weaknesses of its existing collections. These are easily ascertained from the large number of promotional leaflets issued by the organization, and by scanning its journal *Interlending and document supply*.

A list of the materials which BLDSC does not cover reinforces the point that UK libraries need to keep in touch with developments at this major centre. BLDSC does not deal at all with sets of orchestral scores, non-book materials, fiction, 'low level' English language monographs and basic texts, playsets and collections of material for ethnic minorities. It is also useful to know, for instance, that the comprehensive subject coverage of research materials offered since the 1972 British Library Act is not matched by BLDSC's retrospective holdings – which, though unparalleled for science and technology, are much less comprehensive for medicine, the social sciences and the humanities.

More than most areas of professional activity, interlending systems are affected by advances in information technology. Plassard's article *The impact of information technology on document availability and access*[123] usefully summarizes recent developments and predictions.

14 *The book trade*

This book has concentrated on the selection of library materials rather than their acquisition – a subject which is fully treated in books by Chapman[132] for the UK, and Magrill[135] for the United States. It is not always possible to be consistent about separating the two activities. In the section on secondhand books, for instance, contacts with the book trade are so fundamental to the process of selection that both selection and acquisition are described. Similarly for in-print books there are points where library and book trade concerns overlap, and where these have a bearing upon selection they are described below.

In any case it is important that librarians remain in close touch with the industry that produces their raw materials, through the literature, and through formal and informal contacts. A weekly reading of *The bookseller* – 'the organ of the book trade' – is indispensable. Astbury's article[126] surveys recent publications on the trade. The formal contacts between librarians, publishers and booksellers are detailed in Oakeshott's *Liaison in the book world.*[137]

There are a number of bodies on which both the trade and librarians are represented. On the formal side, the National Book Committee (managed from the Book Trust) meets four times a year. Informally, the Working Party of Library and Book Trade Relations is still in existence, though less active than in the 1970s, when it produced a number of valuable publications. The UK Serials Group, formed in 1978, provides a forum for the interchange of ideas between the producers and the end users of serials. The National Acquisitions Group (NAG), established in 1986, aims to promote discussion between all those involved in the acquisition of library materials. From another point of view, a most useful body over the past decade has been the British National Bibliography Research Fund. Established in 1975, the

114

fund aims to stimulate research into all elements of the book world. It has produced several valuable studies which cross library/book trade boundaries, and which are listed in the bibliography of this book. The fund's activities to date are described in a recent article by Greenwood.[47]

Despite the existence of such groups, some of the points of direct contact between libraries, publishers and booksellers are ones that have generated friction. The librarians' grouses include inefficient and lengthy supply procedures, rising prices and publishers' cavalier attitudes to price information. The publishers object to practices such as the reinforcing of paperbacks, and photocopying (especially the activities of the British Library Document Supply Centre). Probably the greatest cause of discontent was the issue of Public Lending Right, only partially defused since some authors began to receive Public Lending Right payments in 1983. Some of this friction arises from genuine conflicts of interest, but some undoubtedly arises from mutual ignorance and misunderstanding.

Leaving aside the areas of conflict, librarians would like to believe that their input to the trade is a vital one. What, then, is their contribution? Statistical analysis of the trade's output has been greatly enhanced by the regular Euromonitor book reports,[130] based upon the government business monitor for books and the Publishers Association's statistics collection scheme. Even so, book trade statistics never quite add up, and can only give an impression rather than an exact picture. In 1988 British publishers' sales were reported as 1,700 million pounds, of which 1,100 million were to individual purchasers, 240 million to 'public institutions' (schools, higher education and public libraries), and a further 360 million estimated to be to 'private institutions' (which include most commercial libraries).

When further broken down, the figures for public institutions are somewhat sobering, since educational libraries represent only 9% of publishers' total sales, and public libraries a mere 5% – and these contributions as a percentage of the total have fallen steadily over the past five years, due to wide-ranging public spending cuts in this period. Librarians point out that for their part they receive fewer volumes for their money, since the prices of books over the same period have risen distinctly faster than retail prices as a whole.

In short, the libraries' contribution to the market makes a

115

substantial enough impact to gain the attention of publishers and booksellers, but not an overwhelming one in relation to overall sales. It is a relatively predictable and reliable feature of the market, but – for the time being, at least – a diminishing contribution. The library performance is better in some types of market than in others. Libraries come nowhere, for instance, in the big selling areas of Bibles, cookery books, dictionaries and classics. On the other hand their impact is very considerable in the market for monographs, quality children's books, and hardback fiction (90% of the sales of which are to public libraries). Finally, as Astbury comments, libraries would claim to contribute the critical component in the market, to provide the counterweight to bestsellerdom, and to contribute substantially to sustaining a wide range of serious books.

Publishers
There are reckoned to be about 2,000 UK publishers who bring out at least one book during any given six month period. The number of large publishers is much smaller – a figure of a few hundred, steadily diminishing as the smaller independent firms are taken over by large conglomerates. The publisher's reputation is an important ingredient in book evaluation, and librarians need to acquire a knowledge of publishing specializations, and of the functions of the various types of publisher (general, specialist, academic, textbooks, university, private press, etc.) and relate these to library requirements. (For instance, librarians should know about and avoid the 'vanity' publishers – firms whose authors pay to have their works published.) Any one publisher's output is usually characterized by a distinctive approach and concentration on certain subject areas. There are several useful directories,[254, 313] and browsing through the catalogues of individual publishers is also informative.

It is also helpful to have some knowledge of trends in publishing. For instance, over the past three decades publishers have tended to produce more titles per year, but smaller numbers of copies of each title. Pryce and Littlechild's *Book prices in the UK*[139] contains the detailed figures. In 1957 UK publishers produced 20,719 titles; in 1967, 29,617; 1977, 36,322; 1985, 52,994; and in 1988, 62,063. But whereas, in 1981, 14,250 books sold for every title published, in 1987 that figure had fallen to 10,913. At the same time, publishers have reduced the size of print runs, to cut down on warehousing costs and other overheads. Although it is difficult to obtain precise information on individual titles, it would now be fairly typical for a general publisher to aim to keep books in print for two years rather than five. Scientific and technical monographs tend to stay in print for a similar length of time, though textbooks may last longer, or be regularly replaced by new editions.

These changes have very real implications for librarians, who must ensure that their initial trawl of new publications is comprehensive, since they are less likely to pick up, through a later stock revision, titles they have initially missed. Librarians must also carefully plan their initial selection decisions to make sure they take place before there is any danger of books being reported out of print (although the chances of a book going out of print in the six months immediately following publication are often exaggerated – this happens rarely, and usually as the result of a miscalculation by the publisher).

Librarians should also keep an eye on book prices, so as to be able to judge what is a fair price for a book – though if a particular title is really wanted there is no option but to pay up. However, it is of interest, for instance, that cost increases in mass market paperbacks during the period 1981 – 6 were almost double those of general hardback publications – a fact which should certainly influence selection choices between hard and paperback editions of the same work.

Booksellers

On the whole, the relationship between booksellers and librarians is a fairly close one – for obvious commercial reasons. The librarian's choice of booksellers has an important effect upon the selection of material as well as upon the speed and efficiency of acquisition. The choice lies essentially between the following groups:

1. library suppliers (booksellers who *only* sell to libraries);
2. large general booksellers;
3. specialist subject booksellers;
4. small local booksellers;
5. secondhand and antiquarian booksellers (see Chapter 18).

It is unusual for a library authority of any size to place all of its orders through one supplier. Most librarians prefer to divide orders amongst a number of booksellers in order to give themselves greater flexibility and a degree of control over the standards of service, and also to make use of the specializations of different dealers. Booksellers also tend to prefer not to be associated exclusively with a few authorities or institutions, so that they themselves are less vulnerable to any changes in those libraries' policies.

To some extent the choice of booksellers depends upon the geographical position of the library and its proximity to a large city. The distribution system of the library suppliers gives them in this sense a considerable advantage. Where a choice is available, however, the librarian will pick his booksellers carefully, trying to gain access through each to some particular advantage: a good shelf stock in certain subjects, from which the librarian may make a personal selection in the shop; a link with the American book trade; a quick service for urgent requests; an agency for required series of foreign books; a technically knowledgeable and reliable staff; an annual sale of slow-selling books at reduced prices.

These are the factors affecting selection. Of course, the acquisition factors are equally important. No bookseller can expect to supply the bulk of a library's orders from stock, and basically the librarian requires a quick, efficient service for material which the bookseller must obtain from the publisher. Speed is sought because readers require books quickly, and because a large number of outstanding orders clogs up the order files, wastes time on reporting, and makes budgeting difficult. Efficiency is also sought in accurate invoicing and supply, regular deliveries and good reporting on outstanding orders. Inaccuracies leading to queries can double the length of time consumed by accessioning routines.

Library suppliers
In several respects the specialist library suppliers differ from general booksellers in the services they are able to offer to libraries. Since their premises are not open to the public, and they do not engage in retail trade, they are able to establish themselves in locations where overheads are cheaper. Sites can be chosen which have expansion potential. Their wide base of trade allows a regular

and prompt delivery service to all parts of the country.

The growth of the library supplier has been a highly significant development of the past 20 years. The number of suppliers doing really substantial amounts of business with libraries is very small. There are just over 100 members of the Library Booksellers Group, but half of these are local retail shops selling to one or two local libraries, whilst others are mainly retail shops with some public library accounts. A much smaller number of companies – perhaps 15 in all – are specialized library suppliers taking 90% of their business from the public library market. A few suppliers have become very large indeed. Glayzer reports[134] that in 1987 four library suppliers were providing approvals services to a total of 194 authorities. (There are only 169 UK authorities, so clearly some were using more than one approval service.) In the amount of business that they do, and the number of services they provide, the library suppliers now play a major role – some would say, too large – in the development of library services.

The services provided have been conveniently listed, both in the paper by John Bunce of JMLS[134] and in Capital Planning Information's recent report *Private process/public advantage: the value to public library authorities of special services provided by library suppliers.*[131] The latter divides services into three groups – supply and financial, processing (generally seen as a form of hidden discount for libraries) and information-related services. It is the third group which concerns us, since it is closely related to selection methods. In effect the 'information-related' services help librarians with selection. The library suppliers maintain showrooms with large stocks, from which visiting librarians may select. They provide 'on approval' collections of new books which librarians may inspect before selecting, and these may either be sent to library premises or – a new development – toured round library authorities in special vans. They provide a wide range of lists and catalogues, including pre-publication lists for new books, tailored stock revision lists, and complete stock lists for standard fiction and children's books. Finally, they provide databases offering online access to extensive files of bibliographical information (up to a million records, in one case).

This is a very wide range of services indeed, and the main responsibility for selection, at least in public libraries, seems to have shifted from library staff to library supplier staff. In fact the library suppliers employ large numbers of library-trained staff – 18 in one firm – to handle this type of work. Although librarians have become accustomed to the situation, the development is an extraordinary one, because the objectives of a public library authority and a library supplier are completely different. The library authority aims to provide the widest possible range of material commensurate with its objectives and the interests of its users. The library supplier aims to make money. In no way can library suppliers be expected to promote a full range of material – not just commercially attractive titles, but also small, low-cost titles from obscure publishers which offer the supplier low profit margins. Yet many librarians seem content to select from a supplier's selection, and to surrender professional responsibility for their service to the suppliers, allowing speed and ease of supply to take precedence over comprehensiveness and depth.

The approval services have put down particularly deep roots. The supplier sends copies of new books (or stock revision collections) to the librarian, who examines them at leisure and decides whether to retain (probably ordering extra copies) or return. The bookseller is recompensed for his trouble with a generous allocation of orders. Most public library authorities, and some academic libraries, now rely heavily on approval collections. Glayzer reports in one survey[134] that 65% of books ordered in a sample from certain public libraries derived from approval collections or visits to booksellers.

The situation seems a bizarre one. There are relatively few circumstances when examination of a book by a librarian can make any significant difference to whether or not the book should be selected for a library – especially so since the biggest consumers of approval collections are public libraries, who do not claim to be experts in any particular field. Can there, for instance, be any meaningful communion in the approval situation between a public librarian and a novel, a biography, a book on plumbing, an introduction to thermodynamics, or even a work on library classification? Few selection decisions are determined by those elements of the book which can only be verified by personal inspection. Nor can there be many librarians who have the time or knowledge to meaningfully sample large portions of the texts of books which are supplied on approval. There is no evidence that books ordered from approval collections are any more successful than books ordered by other methods. In fact Peasgood suggests,[134] in one of the few surveys which have been carried out in this area, that selection in academic libraries from the 'book in hand' was found to be no more effective than selection from lists (effectiveness being measured in terms of subsequent issues).

All bibliographical information provided by suppliers to libraries should be subjected to close scrutiny. Librarians need to know how comprehensive are suppliers' approval collections, databases and listings, and to evaluate how far suppliers' showroom stocks and stock revision lists reflect 'the best' of what is available in print (rather than collections of publishers' cast-offs). Selection of stock should always be dictated by considerations of quality, rather than commercial pressures.

The Net Book Agreement

The Net Book Agreement first came into force after the practice of 'underselling' in the latter half of the nineteenth century had reached a stage where it threatened to undermine the whole of the book trade. The work of a few farsighted publishers and booksellers was responsible for the formulation of an agreement to protect book prices. The wording of the most recent draft of the Net Book Agreement (1957) states that, as a basic rule, 'net books shall not be sold ... to the public at less than the net published prices'. This means that the kind of discount which supermarkets, for example, are able to offer on other consumer goods cannot be applied to books. It is important to remember that the 'net published prices' are those set individually by each publisher for each of his books: they are not a form of collective trade price-fixing.

In 1962 the terms of the Net Book Agreement were upheld following examination in the Restrictive Practices Court, and it was agreed that books were exempt from the terms of the Restrictive Trade Practices Act of 1956. In their judgement the court held that the restrictions implied in the agreement were not contrary to the public interest, that abrogation of the agreement would lead to booksellers being undercut by multiple retail traders and large library suppliers, and that many stockholding booksellers, notably the specialists, would be driven out of business. It was also felt that consequent uncertainty in the bookselling trade would lead booksellers to place smaller initial orders for new titles, and that rising prices and the axing of valuable but commercially marginal titles from publishers' lists would ensue (both of the latter effects have, in fact, to some extent ensued, in spite of the judgement).

Library licence, and book trade economics
The Net Book Agreement allows some relaxation on the matter of discount to libraries that give public access. Booksellers are permitted to give a 10% discount to such libraries, which must first be licensed for this purpose by the Publishers' Association.

In very general terms the trading economics function as follows. The publisher fixes a net price for each book and sells it to the bookseller. The rate of discount which he allows can vary considerably, but the most common discount for general trade books is 35% off the published price. The bookseller must sell to the public at the published price, but may allow 10% discount to the libraries with whom he has a licensing agreement.

Some qualifications to this general rule must immediately be made.

Many publishers give smaller discounts on academic and technical material, usually in the region of 20% to 30% but occasionally lower still. It can be seen that when the bookseller allows a library its full 10% on these titles, his profit will be that much smaller.

'Non-net' books, on which the publisher deliberately refrains from imposing a 'net' price, and which are usually school and other textbooks sold in multiple copies for classroom use, provide another exceptional category. Publishers' discounts are lower than the normal 35% off, and copies sold in the shops or to libraries are usually at the suggested published price. However, booksellers may offer discounts at their own discretion on the sale of multiple copies, the idea being to enable educational authorities to purchase competitively quantities of copies, in supplying which the bookseller does not incur his usual overhead costs because of the volume of the business. In practice the low discounts on non-net books do not give much margin of flexibility.

One further exception is provided by the publisher's practice of 'remaindering' old or unsuccessful titles which have almost stopped selling. In effect, the publisher disposes of the remnant of his edition to one or more dealers at a knock-down price and allows the dealers to sell them at whatever price they like. For many publishers it is a last, unpopular resort for dealing with useless stock. However the quantity of remainders has increased greatly in the last decade, and titles are also being remaindered increasingly quickly to save on overheads (even to the extent of remainder prices being agreed with dealers before publication). Although there may be some pickings for libraries amongst remaindered titles – romantic fiction is an obvious example – non-fiction remainders are only occasionally likely to prove a fruitful source of purchase.

15 *Standards*

This chapter can be skipped by all except readers with a fetish for library standards. Though theoretically useful to library planners and funding authorities, standards rarely seem to have much influence upon events, which are determined by political factors or chance. In recent years there has been more emphasis on the objectives of library services, and less upon quantitative measures. Nevertheless, standards can provide some sort of framework for services, if they are credibly based upon existing practice rather than utopian ideals.

Public libraries

The whole question of the ideal *size* for a public library authority has been a matter of some controversy in Britain since the publication of the McColvin report in 1943.[288] Another significant report appeared in 1961, when the British government appointed a working party to determine the basic requirements for an efficient public library service, with particular reference to authorities of under 40,000 population. The resulting document, the Bourdillon Report,[141] proved at the time to be one of the most useful that had appeared about the bookstocks of British public libraries, since it contained studies of existing provision and a series of recommendations on acceptable standards for provision in the future.

In relation to size of authority, Bourdillon felt that a library authority serving a population of less than 30,000 population would find it difficult to achieve a reasonable standard of bookstock and service. As it happened, the report was overtaken by events, since local authority reorganizations in England and Wales resulted in greatly enlarged units for library and other local government services – between 170,000 to 340,000 population in London, and 250,000 to one million in counties and metropolitan districts.

Another government document – *Public library service points*,[140] published in 1971 – contained further useful recommendations for stock provision in large and small service points within authorities. The report distinguished between two levels of service. Large district libraries with bookstocks of between 40,000 to 100,000 volumes should 'meet the demands of all those whose main need is for books and information on specific subjects, even though they may not be engaged in formal study', and also 'meet the needs of those who wish to select their books from a wide range of cultural or recreational materials of high standard'.

A second level of small, 'in-filling' service points, providing 'a recreational service for adults and a more comprehensive service for children', should carry a total stock of 8,000 volumes.

After size of library authority, and size of library, the matter which is most often addressed by standards is the number of additions to stock per annum. Bourdillon's figure for this was 'the annual provision of not less than 250 volumes for lending and reference purposes per thousand population', but the figure is not as uncomplicated as it seems, since it refers only to new books and not to stock revision (for which no standard was given). The Bourdillon figure relates closely to other standards for public libraries, such as the IFLA recommendation for 1972[142] of 250 volumes per thousand population. The 1986 *Standards for the public library service in Scotland*[144] are slightly more generous, recommending that the 'annual addition to adult lending stock of books and audio-visual materials should be 280 items per 1,000 population'. (Note that the standard excludes reference and children's titles.)

Bourdillon also addressed a question which has remained unaddressed ever since – that is, of the annual output of 24,000 titles (19,000 adult non-fiction) in the *British national bibliography* (*BNB*) at that time, how many should be added to public library stocks? The recommendation was that 5,000 to 6,000 of these were suitable for inclusion in the lending section of any small or middle-sized library, and that the largest libraries would be expected to include almost the whole range of British books, amounting to about 17,000 titles.

In effect, this level of service would have brought authorities close to self-sufficiency, an objective which most experts now agree is unrealistic in view of the very large numbers of titles now published (60,000 annually in the *BNB* alone, compared with the 24,000 of Bourdillon's day), and the speed and efficiency of national interlending services in developed countries.

It would be interesting to know what proportion of new *BNB* titles are ordered by libraries now. Bryant's 1983 article[251] is one of the few pieces of work which touches on the subject, noting the number of selections made by seven public and academic libraries during an eight-week period in 1982. Out of a total of 7,300 *BNB* entries, the libraries ordered 708, 338, 280, 1204, 531, 676 and 653 titles respectively. Two points are immediately apparent. Firstly, there are very big variations in the number of titles added per library. Secondly, the average number of titles selected – 627 – is relatively low, suggesting a very rough total of 4,000 titles per annum from the annual total of 47,000 *BNB* entries for that year.

Academic libraries

Meaningful standards for academic libraries are particularly difficult to devise, because of the wide disparity of existing libraries. The low use rate of many academic libraries (see pp.8 – 10) casts some doubt upon the need for large collections of the kind recommended in standards.

The literature is sparse. Lancaster's book[57] on library evaluation gives some attention to standards. The 1967 University Grants Committee report on British university libraries (the Parry report)[145] contains much information that is still of interest.

Parry envisaged a model budget for materials in a library of 500,000 volumes for a university of 3,000 undergraduates, 1,000 research students and 500 teaching staff. Annual additions recommended for this collection were 16,000 books per annum, 3,000 journal subscriptions p.a., and 4,000 volumes of multiple copies for undergraduate use.

On the matter of size of library budget, Parry commented that a figure of 6% of total university expenditure was 'not a very large proportion in relation to the significance of the library within the university'. It was not clear from the report which items of library expenditure were to be involved in that figure. Staffing *was* included, though a ratio of 50:50 between expenditure on salaries and materials, thought to be reasonable at that time, has since been distorted by a much greater proportion of expenditure going to staffing. For that matter, few British universities have since achieved the 6% figure.

The Canadian Library Association has produced some specific standards[253] which state that the minimum size for a university collection should be 100,000 volumes, to be increased by 20 volumes per graduate student until the standard is overtaken by a different guideline which states that the library should contain 75 volumes per graduate student. Their standards for periodicals are: 1,000 titles for a total student population of 1,000; 4,000 titles for 7,000 students; and 7,250 titles for 13,000 students.

The American Association of College and Research Libraries' *Standards for college libraries*[237] also give some quantitative formulae, suggesting base collections of 85,000 volumes. Another statement covers American university libraries,[238] but does not cite formulae for collections' size or growth rate which can be generally applied. In any case, norms for American university libraries refer to collections which are far larger than in other parts of the world.

The establishment of a new academic library often affords an insight into the way collections measure up to such standards as exist. For instance the government grants made to each of the new British universities in the 1960s, and intended to cover purchase of their basic bookstocks, were estimated by the Parry report to have a purchasing power of 75,000 volumes – less than a third of Parry's recommended figure. Grants to the colleges of advanced technology made at the time of their transition to university status brought the college library stocks up to a similar level. Although the size of all these libraries has since increased, they still fall well below any recommended figures.

Part III

Special materials

16 *Periodicals*

A definition of 'periodical' is taken from Davinson's survey *The periodicals collection*:[150] 'a publication issued under the same title in parts produced at regular intervals and in a sequence with no foreseeable end.' 'Serial' is used synonymously.

Estimates of the number of periodicals published throughout the world vary considerably. Ulrich's *Periodicals directory* – a select list – gives 55,000 titles. The British Library Document Supply Centre has an annual intake of 56,000 titles. Davinson guesses the total figure to be nearer 120,000. Despite the low rate of use of many academic journals (see below), there is no sign of the numbers diminishing. It was estimated in 1989 that scholarly journals were sustaining a net growth in numbers of 3% – 4% per annum. Nor is there any indication yet that the electronic transmission facilities now available for journal articles are leading to reductions in print versions. Woodward argued forcibly[166] in 1987 that a complete switch to electronic transmission from library acquisition of print versions would leave users at a severe disadvantage, by raising overall costs (and therefore diminishing the amount of access), and by removing the facility for quick and easy browsing.

Selection of periodicals
A periodical subscription usually means a substantial recurrent commitment of library funds. It is substantial because periodical prices have risen so steeply in the last decade. It is recurrent because librarians are understandably reluctant to cancel a subscription, once it is placed, and thus devalue their holdings of its back-run. The initial decision to place a subscription should therefore be very carefully considered, and also carefully reviewed at the end of the first year's run – before investment in the title

131

becomes too heavy.

The selection of a *new* periodical title is a particular problem because of lack of information. The appearance of a new periodical title is usually noted in the national bibliography (as it is in the *British national bibliography*) and lists of new serials are also noted in certain periodicals. There are no British equivalents to the American publications *Serials review* and *Choice*, which give reviews of new serials titles through *British book news* contains a regular column on new serials. The selector must largely rely upon his knowledge of the publishing body and editorial board, and on examination of a sample copy of the periodical itself. In this examination he/she will take into account a number of factors: the editorial approach, as reflected in any leading articles; the authority of the contributors; the style and approach of the articles themselves (and in the case of research papers, the clarity and accuracy of the experimental method); the quality of the reviews and correspondence columns; the physical appearance of the journal; the price, in comparison with other journals in the field; and the degree to which the journal makes a fresh contribution in its field when compared with its competitors.

As often as not, the periodicals being considered for purchase are not new ones but established titles. This occurs most frequently – as Woodward's survey notes – when users develop new subject interests, or recommend on request new titles in existing subjects. With established titles a good deal of additional information is likely to be available to aid the selection decision. Lancaster[156] describes a model for weighting the various factors, to gain an overview. The factors are:

1. Soliciting the opinions of users. Views may be sought by interview or questionnaire (see Chapter 5 for detailed information). In an academic library the opinions of faculty are likely to carry some weight, but should be balanced against those of other users.

2. Select lists of journals from an authoritative source. Pages 55 – 9 discuss the use of selective bibliographies (though not all bibliographies include periodicals).

3. Analysis of journals covered by abstracting and indexing services. On the assumption that such services abstract or index only reputable journals, consultation of the list of journals covered

by each service may be of some help to the selector. It is of limited value since no further evaluation of titles is given beyond mere inclusion in the list.

4. Bibliometric analysis. 'Bibliometrics' is the term used to describe the quantitative analysis of behaviour patterns of authors and users. An early and noted bibliometric study resulted in Bradford's 'law of scatter', which found that journals in a subject area could normally be divided into three groups, with each group providing approximately a third of the total number of relevant research papers in the area. The significant point was the size of the groups, since the first contained a very small number of journals, the second five times as many, and the third five times as many again. These findings, which have largely been sustained by subsequent research, offer some practical help to the selector, since they permit the production of *rank lists* of journals in each subject, i.e. journals listed in descending order of importance. Rank lists produced by Bradford's method will tend to begin with a small core of essential titles and end with a long tail of fringe titles which becomes increasingly irrelevant.

Two other bibliometric methods are commonly employed to lead to the production of rank lists. These are: 1) citation analysis, and 2) the analysis of interlending records of large libraries. Citation analysis – a very prominent bibliometric technique – consists of the analysis of the lists of references which appear at the end of most scholarly papers. The assumption is that frequently cited papers are the most important in the literature. A common corollary is analysis of the journal titles which contain the cited articles, and thence the ranking of these titles in order of importance (viz., frequency of citation). The method can reasonably claim to give some indication of important journals in a subject literature, though of course citation of an article is no guarantee that it is read – and indeed Scales's study[163] suggests that citation analysis is not in fact a very accurate guide to use.

Most rank lists from citation analysis are in any case too short to be of much use. The longest are those in the annual cumulation of *Science citation index* (since 1975) and *Social sciences cumulation index* (since 1977).

The third method of producing rank lists of journals is by

analysis of the interlending (or photocopying) records of a large lending library. The method tends to highlight the journals which are commonly agreed to be the most important in their field, though at first sight this may seem a little curious (since 'borrowing' libraries might be expected to hold the core journals in stock and borrow more peripheral titles).

The British Library Document Supply Centre (BLDSC) is an obvious example of a library whose records are worth analysing, and has in fact carried out several surveys, including a major one in 1980 reported by Clarke.[149] (At this time the library was called the British Library Lending Division (BLLD).) Clarke found, for instance, that from the library's total holdings of 54,000 journals, 45% of all requests for journal articles were satisfied from 2,000 journals, and 80% from 7,500 journals. Such findings have obvious implications for the selection of periodical titles elsewhere, but should nevertheless be interpreted with caution. Kefford and Line, in a subsequent article,[154] reported considerable variations between the 1980 survey and a previous BLLD survey carried out in 1976, and advised that those using rank lists for the determination of smaller core collections locally should try to allow for local subject biases in demand.

More question marks are raised, again by Line,[158] in an article comparing the consistency over similar periods of time of the rank lists produced from interlending data with those produced from citation analysis. The comparison shows striking differences, with citation-based lists holding up much better over a period time – e.g. the overlap in the top 100 titles of the citation-based analysis was 95% at its most extreme (cf. 57% for the interlending-based surveys) and 78% at its least extreme (cf. 56%). What this proves is uncertain. Citations are principally used by academics, and citation-based lists are clearly more reliable for academic collections. Interlending-based lists are drawn from records of actual use from a wide range of clients, with academic and commercial/industrial users roughly equal. Line suggests that more research is required into the whole area.

One other limitation affects all rank lists, whatever their method of production. The core journals in any subject field rarely amount to more than half a dozen, and these are usually clearly identified by rank lists. However, the findings relating to peripheral journals – on which the selector particularly needs guidance – tend to be unreliable because their rate of citation (interlending, etc.) is relatively low.

Works by Meadows[159] and by Rowley and Turner[162] include clear summaries of developments in bibliometric studies, together with further guidance to the extensive literature in this field.

In conclusion it may be said that bibliometric analyses are useful, and potentially extremely valuable, for selection purposes. However they also contain a number of traps for the unwary, and need to be carefully evaluated with local circumstances in mind.

Cancellation and relegation of periodicals

Funding shortages frequently oblige librarians to cancel periodical subscriptions, whilst shortages of space oblige them to relegate back-runs of titles to reserve stock or remote storage. In either case hard decisions have to be made. Use of the stock is the most important (though by no means the only) factor to be taken into account when resolving which titles have to go.

Use of periodicals takes two distinct forms. Firstly, current awareness use of the latest issues, usually in-house, keeps researchers up-to-date in their subject areas. Secondly, reference to specific articles from back-runs takes place, either in-house or from a loaned copy of the relevant issue of the journal. Because periodicals are essentially vehicles for new information, the current awareness function is probably the more important, and because this takes place in-house it is more difficult to measure than – for instance – the use of books from loan records. Perhaps for this reason, studies of periodical use in libraries are relatively rare compared with those of book use.

Nevertheless, the studies that have been carried out, especially in academic libraries, often reveal fairly low levels of use – or rather, intensive use of a small number of core journals, and low use of a much larger number of peripheral titles. The University of Pittsburgh study,[155] for instance, found that over periods of 39 – 80 hours the percentage of the periodicals collection used in different faculties was: physics 37%; life sciences 12%; engineering 7%; chemistry 15%; mathematics 85%. It was estimated that 55% of the titles in engineering, and 25% of the titles in physics, received less than five uses per annum, and that in all only 10% of the journals held were consulted more than 100 times a year.

A number of methods have been devised to study the in-house use of periodicals. These include:

1. Counting periodicals left lying on reading tables, on the assumption that they were previously taken from the shelf to be consulted.

2. Removing periodicals from the open shelf sequence and counting resulting enquiries for them.

3. Attaching forms to the periodicals themselves, and asking users to note each consultation.

4. Interviewing users to ask which periodicals they consult. Horwill describes[166] an extension of this method used in the University of Sussex, where all lecturers, research workers and postgraduate students were allowed to vote for titles they wanted to retain.

5. Observing periodical display shelves over a period of time, and recording all consultations made. (For accurate results with this method, periodicals must be returned to display shelves immediately after use.)

Of these, method 5 (observation) gives by far the most accurate guide to use, as long as it is carried out over a sufficient period of time – although it absorbs more staff time than other methods. Methods 1 – 4 are all likely to lead to substantial inaccuracies in the picture they give of in-house use, with 1 – 3 recording a short-fall, and 4 probably registering an over-estimate. Surprisingly, method 3 appears to be the one most commonly used.

The sharp rises in periodical prices during the past decade, coupled with a decline in library funding, have meant that university and special librarians have found an increasing proportion of their budgets being absorbed by periodical subscriptions, to the detriment of the bookstock, and to a point where cutting of subscriptions became inevitable. For most university librarians, cuts on such a scale were a new experience. Blake and Meadows[147] describe how this experience affected 33 UK academic libraries in a survey carried out in 1983. During the period 1974 – 82, most of the libraries had had to make some periodical cuts. The situation was particularly bad in the 1980s, with an average number of 358 titles per university discontinued during the period 1980 to mid-1983. Decisions on cuts were largely taken by the academic staff, though the process was often orchestrated by librarians. Two-thirds of the libraries had carried out use surveys. The most commonly cited characteristics of journals cut were high price, large price increases, and foreign language content. (Additional characteristics cited in an earlier survey by Woodward[312] were: duplicate titles; titles for which a second subscription was held in a neighbouring institution; titles in which the subject approach adopted was too general, or too specialized; periodicals in which the content overlapped with other journals held in stock.)

One-third of the libraries in the Blake and Meadows survey said that 'other things being equal' they would cancel journals from commercial publishers before those produced by learned societies. The reasons most commonly cited for retention of journals were frequent use, high academic value and high relevance to teaching and research in the university. Half the respondents said that 'other things being equal' they would retain journals with longer back-runs in the library.

New subscriptions during this period were said to be made either by cancelling subscriptions of comparable price, or by taking money from the bookfund.

Linked to the need for the cancellation of periodical subscriptions are decisions on the relegation of back-runs of periodicals to remote storage – though in this case the limitation of service is forced not directly by lack of funding but by lack of space in the library building. Buckland has discussed[148] the need to observe the use of the entire run of each journal in stock so as to estimate the benefit of investment in continued retention and compare this against remote storage costs. (He also considers the timing of periodical binding in relation to patterns of use.) Fussler and Simon found[151] that 'the use of volumes within the same serial is closer than the amount of use of volumes chosen randomly from other serials'.

Unfortunately, few university libraries keep regular records of in-house use of serials, and since it is estimated that in-house use may be five times as great as that recorded by loan statistics this means that there is rarely a real basis for decision making. In any case the equation between retention and relegation to storage cannot be put with any exactness since the effects upon users of withdrawing immediate access to journals is not known. Taylor and Urquhart noted[164] that the cheapest way of identifying

137

periodical titles for relegation is to make use of data taken from BLDSC records on little-used material, and that for scientific journals (but not for medical) this compared well with other methods for 'accuracy' and 'prediction'.

General studies of obsolescence have as yet provided little information of practical use to the librarian for making decisions on the relegation of back-runs of periodical titles (see p.89). Line and Sandison, in their review of obsolescence studies,[157] conclude that it is probably more cost effective to discard whole runs of less-used journals than to discard the older volumes of all serials taken (thus supporting Fussler and Simon's findings). They therefore recommend that the librarian having to discard or relegate back-runs of journals should identify:

1. journals which are dead (not now taken, or ceased publication);
2. journals which receive little use of current issues;
3. journals for which use falls off dramatically after three years (after which time there is normally a rapid fall-off in the use of journals, especially in scientific fields).

Where shortage of space (rather than of recurrent funding) is the main motivation for discarding periodical runs, some research libraries have adopted the approach of microfilming the originals before discard.

Exchange
The practice of acquiring library materials by offering on exchange publications of the parent body usually relates to serials. Once quite a common way of acquiring periodicals, it has lost favour because analyses of the costs of staff time, postage, etc. have suggested that it is cheaper or almost as cheap to buy outright. It is, too, a method that tends to be misused, the notion that a publication is free overruling evaluation of its potential use to the library. Nevertheless it is sometimes the only way of acquiring certain foreign journals from countries where there are currency exchange problems or where the organization of the book trade does not allow the regular despatch of serials.

Periodicals in public libraries
Most of the above relates principally to primary journals and their

use in academic and special libraries. The provision of periodicals in public libraries is on a considerably smaller scale. Oldman and Davinson's survey[160] estimated that 4.2% of the average public library's bookfund was spent on periodicals. The same survey noted the lack of a periodical policy in public libraries and the poor definition of user needs, but established nevertheless that certain categories of serial were considered important by the libraries' clienteles, and were used. In particular Oldman and Davinson observed a relatively heavy use of national and local newspapers, journals on hobbies and subjects of practical interest, and trade and technical journals, and that this type of use was fairly constant despite variations locally in provision. In sharp contrast to periodical use in special and university libraries, most of the interest expressed was current and general in nature. Sixty-three per cent of respondents said that their use was not specific in any way; 66% did not consult back numbers of periodicals.

Despite the fact that it involves relatively little expenditure, periodical provision in public libraries should not be taken too lightly. Luckham observed[274] that 11% of all respondents in his survey consulted newspapers, and 12% periodicals. Thirty-five per cent of the periodical readers in the Oldman and Davinson survey were not members of the library authority (and so, presumably, did not borrow books); 68% claimed to consult certain titles on a regular basis. It seems likely that there is a small but faithful periodical clientele, some of whom may not be attracted to the library for any other reason. Unfortunately few public library authorities are as yet informed as to what this clientele consists of, or what its requirements are.

139

17 *Foreign language materials*

Special problems connected with the provision of foreign language material can be addressed within three categories – provision for research, provision for immigrant communities, and provision of popular classics for general reading or study.

Provision for research
Much of the demand from university and special libraries is for material required for research purposes. The researcher does not normally wish to read in a foreign language *per se*: he is obliged to do so by the fact that the relevant research findings are not available in any other language. Provisions of such material raises a number of intractable problems, including those relating to selection and acquisition.

Recent surveys have tried to quantify the amount of foreign language literature relevant to research needs.[172, 173] Anything between 20% – 70% of references in abstracting services are to articles published in languages other than English. Overall, the most important research languages, after English, seem to be French, German, Russian and Japanese – in descending order of importance, though considerable variations are apparent when particular languages are related to specific subject fields. (For instance, a relatively high proportion of research workers in dentistry deem German and Japanese literature important; a relatively low proportion of research workers in medicine refer to Russian literature, despite its importance in other scientific fields.) Each subject field must therefore be regarded separately according to user needs.

The surveys referred to have also shown quite clearly that language barrier problems have prevented a great many research workers from consulting relevant literature. For instance, only with French do British research workers appear to have attained a reasonable command of another language. From a 'selection' point of view, it is sometimes suggested that lack of use of foreign language works should not lead automatically to cuts in materials, but rather that measures should be taken to overcome the language barrier itself. A wide range of solutions have been put forward – improvement of language qualifications amongst research workers, more cover-to-cover translation of journals, better and more widely publicized translation agencies, fuller English language abstracts of articles – some of them pursued, without notable success.

In the circumstances individual university and special libraries tend to cut down on their holdings of foreign language books and periodicals and lean more heavily on the national interlending system. However, even on a national scale requests for such material meet with mixed success. British library holdings of foreign language journals, for instance, are fairly comprehensive, but holdings of monographs are extremely patchy despite increases in the rate of acquisition since the formation of the British Library. With a wide scatter in demand, and little duplication of demand for individual titles, there are apparently insoluble difficulties facing any attempt to rationalize national coverage of foreign-language materials.

For the individual university or special library the difficulties of selection of foreign language books are hard to separate from those of acquisition – both depending upon the state of bibliographical control and book trade information in the country concerned. It has been estimated, very approximately, that over half of the books produced internationally are published in nine or ten countries, and while the proportion of literature from developing countries may be expected to increase steadily in the near future, there is clearly a case at the present time for adopting a special approach – based on printed bibliographical sources – to acquiring books from countries with highly developed book trades.

In developing countries the inadequacy of printed bibliographical resources causes problems. A useful working tool entitled *Acquisition and provision of foreign books by national and university libraries in the UK*[167] outlines the problems of acquisition for particular regions of the world, and suggests some of the solutions to these.

Several writers refer to the problems caused by delays in the appearance of national bibliographies, particularly when related to short print runs. Outside the developed countries, few national bibliographies achieve a comprehensive coverage. (The accessions lists of the local Library of Congress offices are often considered to provide a fuller listing.) The lack of selective bibliographies is another serious problem. Some British and American librarians use as their main selection tool the accessions list of a major home-based library specializing in the same field.

The most common alternative to selection from lists and bibliographies is the commissioning of an agent in the country concerned to make a selection of new books on the library's behalf, according to a carefully prepared brief. Such an arrangement necessitates a good deal of confidence in the agent. Dilution of the agent's responsibility may be achieved by requiring him to submit a list of recommendations, from which the librarian makes the choice. Personal contact between librarian and agent is highly desirable if a system closely tailored to the library's needs is to be achieved.

The interchange of publications between libraries of institutions or universities in different countries is often adopted as a means of avoiding financial commitment and currency exchange difficulties.

Immigrant communities

Some British public library authorities receive heavy demand for foreign language materials for immigrant communities. Polish, Greek and Turkish are prominent amongst the European languages required. Perhaps the largest demand comes from British people of Asian origin, with Bengali, Punjabi, Gujurati and Sanskrit prominent, amongst a number of other languages. Demand is particularly heavy in certain areas, notably London and the Midlands.

The first serious study of immigrant reading requirements in UK was by Clough and Quarnby[168] in 1978. Since that time provision for immigrant groups has certainly improved, although there remains much to be done. Two studies by Elliott[170, 171] indicate some of the problems.

In preparing for provision of this kind each authority needs to carry out its own assessment of needs. These vary considerably.

As far as generalization is possible, the main demand is for fiction and for material covering the politics, religion and culture of the immigrant groups. Provision can cause obvious difficulties for library staff unfamiliar with the language or culture, but the trend in the past decade has been for authorities to appoint ethnic librarians who are familiar with needs (and with the required languages).

One problem, as with all areas of minority provision, is maintaining freshness of stock in what is a relatively small collection. Mobility of stock is essential, through exchanges between service points in the same authority, and – for some languages – through loan collections (changed periodically), from an outside cooperative scheme. The two major collections of this kind in Britain are the Library of Asian Languages at Birmingham Public Libraries, and the Polish Central Circulating Library in London.

Bibliographical information is another problem, rarely solved by recourse to national bibliographies from overseas or other printed lists. Many libraries lean heavily on selection by UK-based specialist booksellers who import materials from abroad and whose numbers have greatly increased over the past decade. Booksellers based abroad are also used. Elliott reports[170] an increase in UK indigenous publishing for ethnic minority groups, identifying 105 publishers, in a large number of different languages, and guessing that at least 200 more publishers are in existence. The publishing output however is small – he records 27 publishers producing a total of 354 book titles in the course of five years. Elliott lists 40 specialist bookshops, together with many magazines giving advertisements for a wide variety of publications. He estimates that perhaps 50% of UK published book titles appear in the *British national bibliography* or *The bookseller*.

Many of these books – whatever their source – are poorly produced, and require reinforced binding before being placed upon library shelves.

Popular classics
British public libraries normally provide a limited range of material for users who wish to read in a foreign language *per se*, rather than to obtain information which only happens to be available in a foreign language. Users of this material consist largely of

British nationals who are either studying a language and require back-up material, or who have in the past achieved fluency in a language and enjoy reading it. The content of such collections is largely fiction, poetry and drama, though classic works of biography, history, etc. are also included. Some edited versions of texts may be provided. Most British libraries restrict provision of this kind to the major European languages, with French and German most prominent.

Marcan provides some useful practical information on building up collections of this kind.[169] Libraries need to hold the basic bibliographies for the major European languages, together with surveys of those literatures. There are several reputable foreign language booksellers in Britain willing to offer valuable advice and guidance, with Grant & Cutler (London) outstanding amongst them. *World literature today* (formerly *Books abroad*) is a valuable reviewing journal in this area, and recourse may also be had to specialist reviewing journals of the countries themselves. Care should be taken to stock the most important prizewinning books in the major European languages. Mobility of stock within each authority is essential if a range of new titles is to be made regularly available to the minority clientele.

18 Out-of-print materials

Ranganathan states that in a 'service' library there is no place for books selected for their 'oldness of physique'.[297] If this is accepted, then the private collector's interest in acquiring books according to their rarity, reputation, physical condition, provenance (previous whereabouts) or the fluctuations of fashion have no direct part to play in a librarian's selection. The 'service' librarian acquires books so that his users may consult them, and the user's interest is normally in the *intellectual* content of the book, rather than in its rarity as such.

Rarity is, of course, a relative concept. Any out-of-print book is rare in that it is more difficult to obtain than a work which is 'in print', and (usually) more expensive. The condition of 'rarity' as defined by a 'rare' bookseller depends primarily upon the size of the book's original edition and subsequent fluctuations in the work's reputation, and also upon demand. A work may be difficult to find but if it is not sought by collectors it cannot be described as 'rare'. A great many works are 'out of print' but if there are still large numbers of copies in circulation they would merely be described as 'out-of-print' or 'secondhand'. Some of the books sought by librarians fall into this category, and their acquisition does not create the special problems connected with rare book librarianship. Libraries which do have substantial collections of 'rare' books normally employ specially qualified staff to manage them, since the knowledge and skills required for rare book librarianship are different from those required for treating conventional library materials.

All types of library have occasion, at one time or another, to search for out-of-print books to add to their stock. For librarians from universities or learned societies the selection and acquisition of out-of-print material forms an important and recurrent feature of their work. Some public libraries – notably in the large cities – also have outstanding collections of rare books. These are the exceptions rather than the rule, though every public library authority periodically needs to acquire out-of-print books for local history collections, or to make good omissions which for one reason or another have become apparent in the stock.

For library purposes, out-of-print books may be purchased in one of three ways: by visiting secondhand bookshops, by marking up dealers' catalogues, or by preparing desiderata lists to submit to dealers.

Dealers may be broadly classified into the rare book specialists, and those who deal with the whole gamut of secondhand books whatever their price or vintage. Where time and circumstances permit, regular visits to both categories of dealer usually prove worthwhile. They afford an opportunity to examine stock on the booksellers' shelves, and they also strengthen the librarian's hand in bidding for stock for which other customers are also in the market. To capitalize on visits of this kind the librarian needs an excellent knowledge of his own stock.

In addition to visiting dealers, the librarian will also ask to receive dealers' catalogues, as and when these are appropriate to his needs. Catalogues list materials which have come into the dealer's possession recently (sometimes in the form of a large special collection) and which are being offered for sale. The catalogue quotes the book's bibliographical details, the price, and – in the case of rare books – gives an indication of physical condition.

The crucial requirement in checking dealers' catalogues is speed. They must be read through immediately upon receipt, and checked against the library's desiderata file where necessary, and orders should be telephoned through immediately to the dealer. Delay invariably means that some of the works listed are taken by other customers.

A 'desiderata' file is the library's list of wants – titles previously sought for one reason or another and found to be out-of-print. The list should note the title and bibliographical details of each book, when it went out of print, the reason it is required and its importance to the library, and a note of any action taken so far. It has already been noted that desiderata lists may be checked against dealers' catalogues. The librarian may also take the more positive step of sending his desiderata list to one or more dealers, with instructions to search for the titles on behalf of the library. After checking his own holdings the dealer advertises for the wanted titles – in the United Kingdom this is usually done through the weekly journal called *The clique* – and refers back to the librarian with details of the price and condition quoted. (Alternatively, the librarian may suggest automatic purchase below a given price.) While not obliged to purchase works identified by the dealer, most librarians would regard themselves as morally bound to do so as long as the price and condition of the work are reasonable. The use of a single dealer, rather than several, is usually preferred, to avoid multiple advertising for the same titles. The dealer should be given a reasonable period – at least six months – to track down the titles.

The desiderata file of a British university might typically run to some 2,000 items. The file should be periodically revised, in association with academic staff, to see whether listed items are still wanted or (by checking against the library catalogue) have in fact already been added to stock. An article by Cameron and Roberts describes[174] how the file in Dundee University was revised and subsequently automated to facilitate further revision.

Ground rules for putting a *price* on an out-of-print book cannot be definitely stated. A useful guideline can be taken from reference books which record the actual prices registered in recent sales.[248] But judgement of 'a fair price' depends upon a number of factors in addition to rarity, and the records of other sales – if taken without due consideration of the background details – can be very deceptive. Fashions in book buying come and go. The condition of a book, and its provenance, can both have a considerable influence upon price. The buyer is advised to enter each transaction with a good knowledge of both dealer and book so as to avoid paying a badly inflated price for an inferior product. (It should be noted that secondhand copies of books, whether in print or not, are in no way subject to the conditions of the Net Book Agreement.)

The *condition* of a rare or secondhand book is less important to a librarian than to a private collector. Roderick Cave, in his *Rare book librarianship*[175] defines 'good condition' in a book as 'complete and undisturbed in its original binding ... and clean and sound throughout'. In view of the fact that the condition of

147

a library copy of a book – if it is used at all – will soon decline, the purchase of slightly inferior copies is justified, and may achieve a considerable overall saving on prices.

Lists of dealers, together with their specializations, are available from a number of sources. In addition to the general dealers in rare books and secondhand books, there are specialist booksellers for most subject areas. Experience over a period of time will show which dealers offer an efficient service, and if more than one dealer is used a record should be kept enabling the librarian to compare the proportion of titles supplied from wants lists, the average delay in supply, etc.

Donations

All types of library are liable to receive unsolicited donations of material from time to time, varying in size from a handful of books to large and important special collections (the latter often forming a notable part of university and research library collections).

An offer of a really large collection raises major policy issues for consideration at a high level within the institution concerned. But to some extent the issues involved differ only in scale from those raised by any proposed donation. Is the donation suitable for the library? Will it be used? (A survey by Diodata and Diodata in a medium-sized academic library[258] found that purchased books circulated four times more often than donations.) Can the material be properly housed and indexed? Are there any special limitations attached to the gift, and if so is the library prepared to meet them? If these questions cannot be resolved, then librarians should be prepared to redirect donors to other locations – mindful of the high cost of maintaining special collections, which may require extra security, air conditioning, and separate reading rooms and exhibition areas. Cox's article 'Rare books and special collections'[176] gives a valuable account of how this aspect of a university librarian's work is managed in practice.

19 Paperbacks

Paperbacks are big business in the British book trade, accounting for 40% of total cash sales. A majority of paperbacks still appear a year or so after their hardbound versions, but since 1980 the traditional pattern of publishing has diversified to an unprecedented extent, with quite a large number of paperbacks coming out simultaneously with their hardbacks, or as paperback orginals. The most significant development has been the so-called 'trade' or 'B-format' paperbacks, midway between hardback and paperback in price and print run, and also in appearance, since they are generally larger than traditional paperbacks and better produced, with stiffer covers. They come either from hardback houses or from paperback publishers under separate imprints (such as Picador from Pan, or Abacus from Sphere).

It used to be the case that libraries wanting to select a particular title would purchase the hardback edition where one existed, and the paperback where it did not. Recent surveys by Capital Planning Information[13] and by Hart[178] reveal changed attitudes, with some public libraries making it a matter of policy to purchase paperbacks *per se* in considerable numbers. Hart, examining the proportion of printed volumes bought as paperbacks in 27 library authorities, described a wide variety in the scale of provision. The bulk of authorities fell into two fairly equal groups, one group stating that paperbacks took up a mere 3% – 5% of total provision, the other between 20% – 30%. Many of these paperbacks, intended for recreational reading, were purchased in bulk (taking advantage of minimal invoicing and accessioning procedures), reinforced, and placed on library shelves uncatalogued.

Two main reasons were given for the large-scale provision. The first – economy, because of cuts in bookfunds – is somewhat

149

controversial. Hart's survey recorded fairly general agreement that two to three years and 30 issues was the average longevity of a paperback in use in public libraries. Against this must be reckoned the much greater longevity of the hardback, not to mention the requirement to withdraw and reorder paperbacks which have worn out. It is unlikely that in the long term paperbacks do present the more cost-effective option. Paperback afficionados should also take into account Pryce and Littlechild's finding[139] that in the period 1981 – 6 the prices of mass market paperbacks doubled in comparison with hardback prices. In other words, paperbacks are no longer such a bargain on straight cost comparisons.

The second reason given for large-scale provision of paperbacks was the visual appeal of the format to some groups of people – in particular, the young. Again, the assertion is disputable. For no discernible reason, some public librarians seem to have undertaken a crusade in favour of paperback provision. Cropper's tendentious paper[257] is characteristic of this approach, in citing evidence in favour of paperback provision but omitting to mention evidence against. In fact, the few surveys which have studied user attitudes to paperback provision in libraries have all found in favour of hardbacks. One survey of fiction use[194] reported 56% of users in favour of hardback formats, 8% in favour of paperbacks, and 36% 'don't mind's'. Goodall[182] reports her own survey, which found 40% preferences for hard format and 17% for paper, and also a survey by Steptoe, who found 28% in favour of hardback fiction and 11% for paper. And Harrison's survey[177] found 50% in favour of hardback, 24% in favour of paperback.

If there is no automatic mandate for large-scale provision of paperbacks in libraries, there are certainly circumstances when the purchase of paperback titles is obligatory. This happens most often when a title is only available in paperback – as is the case, for instance, with an increasingly large number of classic works of literature, as well as new titles of all kinds. All librarians are bound to buy large numbers of paperback titles which fall into this category. There are also cases when it is genuinely more cost effective to take the paper rather than the hardback option – for instance, with a reference book which is likely to be infrequently used, and where the price difference between hard and paper editions is very large, or to satisfy short-term demand with extra copies which can be discarded as soon as their immediate purpose is served.

One other factor has a bearing. Paperback publishers have long been displeased with the library practice of reinforcing their products, and few paperbacks appear without a printed warning on the reverse of the title page forbidding such reinforcement – a warning so far widely ignored without penalty. Where titles are only available in paperback editions the publishers' attitude on reinforcement seems unreasonable, not to say counter-productive. On the other hand, large-scale purchasing and reinforcing of paperbacks which are also available in hardback seems to be a case of librarians behaving unreasonably.

20 *Fiction*

Fiction reading

Reading fiction is a widespread activity in Britain, and fiction provision is the public library's largest and probably its most important service. We now know a good deal more than we did 10 years ago about the fiction reading habits – library and non-library – of the British public. The broadest picture is provided every two years by the highly informative Euromonitor surveys.[130] For instance, in answer to the question, 'Are you reading a book at the time of this survey?', 45% of Euromonitor's 1988 sample responded 'yes'. Of the affirmatives, 69% were reading a novel, whilst 28% reported reading a work of non-fiction. (Since 7% of the 28% were reading biography, and a further 6% history, a high proportion of the total were reading 'for pleasure' rather than purposively.) The 69% reading fiction broke down: romance 17%; thriller 14%; war/adventure 4%; historical 7%; modern novel 10% (this last a large increase on previous years).

Answers to the survey question 'How did you obtain the book you are reading?' gave the public library service no cause for complacency, since 37% of respondents had bought the book they were reading, 33% had borrowed from a library, 17% had borrowed from a friend, and 7% were reading gifts. An aggregation of 'bought' and 'gift' columns brings purchases out well ahead of public library borrowing as a source of fiction reading, even though the former affects the reader's pocket, whilst the latter is free.

There have been several recent studies of the use of fiction in public libraries. Dixon's book *Fiction in libraries*[181] includes detailed information on loan statistics. Surveys by Spiller[194] and Sear and Jennings[191] look at fiction use, while Goodall's invaluable 'Browsing in public libraries'[182] summarizes the findings of eight user surveys. Finally John Sumsion, Registrar of Public Lending Right, has published detailed tables of his organization's statistics[195] which refer to use of fiction and non-fiction in a large number of libraries.

The first point to note from these surveys is that fiction takes up a remarkably large proportion of the total issues of public libraries. Dixon reports that on average fiction absorbs 72% of total issues, and 65% of the total material *on loan* at any one time (whilst on average comprising the lower figure of 45% of total adult lending stock).

Spiller's survey broke down fiction loans in some detail, finding that 79% of them could broadly be classified as recreational, 21% 'serious' (for want of a better word). Further breakdown of the 79% of recreational reading differed from that of the Euromonitor survey, viz.: thriller/mystery 27%; adventure 10%; romance 13%; historical romance 10%; 'family story' 10%; science fiction 6% (the differences probably caused by Euromonitor's coverage of purchasing as well as borrowing).

In addition to revealing what fiction users read, the various surveys also discover a good deal about the way people choose fiction from libraries. As this is information which librarians can use to select and exploit fiction stock more effectively, it is analysed in some detail below.

The most significant findings to emerge from all the surveys concerned the importance of *browsing* as a way of searching for fiction, and the importance to users of discovering *authors* whose works they like. Users seem to be about equally divided between these two strategies. The browsing process itself is often used to allow the reader to come across known authors, though it is also used to choose books where the author is not known (the latter often constituting the surprising high proportion of 40% – 50% of total choices). Despite the popularity of browsing, novels chosen by this method were found by Sears and Jennings to be less likely to be enjoyed than novels chosen by the author approach. Specifically, those selecting by browsing had only 'positively enjoyed' one out of three novels chosen, whilst those selecting known authors had 'positively enjoyed' four out of five. The message is clear and disconcerting.

The hunt for new authors is the most persistent activity of fiction readers in public libraries, as all those who have carried out user

153

surveys confirm. 'I liked the author's other books' is constantly cited as a motive for choice. Authors' names are also important for the sizeable numbers of people (between 14% to 29% in four different surveys) who select fiction from libraries on behalf of others. Yet the overwhelming impression is that a majority of users do not know how to find new authors. Most users have a small list of favourites – often names discovered years earlier – and are at a loss if they cannot find books by any of these authors on the shelves. Spiller's report of a man of 30 who knew only two authors – Edgar Wallace and G. K. Chesterton – both recommended by his mother, poignantly symbolizes a fairly common sense of helplessness.

Yet public libraries do little to assist the search for new authors, and their 'failure at the shelf' rate is probably unacceptably high, disguised by the high level of substitutability which is possible in this field. Three surveys summarized by Goodall reported 43%, 52% and 54% of users respectively searching unsuccessfully for authors. Oddly, in view of these figures, few fiction readers use the reservation system (about 1% of fiction issued is obtained by reservation), and very few complain about the service.

What else is to be learnt from these surveys, and what practical measures can public librarians take to improve performance in the area? There is something to be gained from studying the way that users browse. For instance, only one person in three refers to the text when browsing, which seems to suggest that for most readers literary style is not a preoccupation. One in five claim to be influenced by the title or the design of the cover. Small print is a minor but noticeable deterrent to choice, for poorly-sighted readers (for whom the large-print series are a valuable addition to public libraries), but also for normally-sighted readers. A factor affecting many users (29% in one survey) is the height of the library shelves – both high and low shelves being ruled out by a gamut of medical conditions. This is a finding which *can* be acted upon, and clearly libraries should avoid extremes of shelving for bookstocks where browsing is a major feature in user selection of titles.

By far the largest factor in selection by browsing is the blurb, with up to 80% of users rating blurbs as important. Whilst most librarians regard blurbs as highly dubious instruments for choosing a novel, they should nonetheless see that the blurbs are retained on the covers of all copies of novels in stock.

The age of fiction is also a factor in use. As might be expected, user preferences are for more recently published novels. Sumsion found that 55% of loans in 20 libraries derived from books published in the previous five years (34% of the total stock); 26% of loans from the 24% of stock which was 6 – 10 years old; 11% of loans from 18% of stock 11 – 15 years old. The figures show the need for a constant supply of new titles, though older material is by no means neglected by the public.

It is clear from a variety of sources that the A – Z fiction sequence in libraries is unhelpful when users do not have a clear idea of what they want. Many public libraries now categorize fiction on the shelves (see the section on light fiction below). Another very important source of user choice is the returned books area. The Sear and Jennings survey found that 46% of the books studied in their sample had come from this section. The figure may seem astonishingly high to librarians, but suggests that users seek the reassurance of choosing from a smaller area than the main sequence, and one where every title has recently been read (though not necessarily enjoyed) by another user. The inescapable corollary is that libraries should not reshelve returned books immediately they are received. In fact if the area is in such demand, returned books should probably be left in an easy access area for at least a day before being returned to the main A – Z sequence.

On a similar track, the importance of fiction display has been thoroughly explored by Sear and Jennings, who took the admirable and unusual step of investigating a problem in one piece of research, and a solution in a second. *Novel ideas: a browsing area for fiction*[192] describes the setting up of public library browsing areas, in which stock was arranged under a number of themes intended to help users choose their fiction. The exercise made heavy use of staff time, but the results were largely positive. Some 40% of people interviewed said they had found the area easier to use than the A – Z sequence, and the satisfaction with books chosen was higher than the authors had found in previous research. (On the other hand, 30% of interviewees said they had not even noticed the area, drawing attention to the need to publicize any departures from established and traditional systems.) This initiative on display deserves to be widely followed up in public libraries.

Most research suggests that library booklists are *not* found very helpful by users, because of frustrations in locating books recommended in the lists. One survey found that users were influenced by books recommended or serialized on TV or radio (20% and 13%, respectively, of those surveyed), suggesting that librarians need to keep in touch with the media's treatment of fiction. The weekly *Books in the media* (published in Chesham, Bucks.) does just this for booksellers (though the publication is little known by librarians), listing radio and TV mentions of books for the week following publication, and press reviews for the previous week. Another idea worth pursuing – though rarely seen so far in libraries – is one adopted by Peter Mann's *Reader's guide to fiction authors*[188] and the more recent *Bloomsbury good reading guide*,[184] which link like titles with like so that readers are guided through a network of novels similar in style and/or content.

Finally, only a very small proportion of users are accustomed to asking library staff for help in choosing fiction (16% and 4% in two surveys which addressed this question). Reasons included the personal nature of fiction selection, but also the unapproachability of staff, low expectations, and the perception that fiction was an unimportant service and therefore not appropriate for using up staff time. It is probable that librarians do little to dispel this last perception. Yet in view of the sheer quantity of fiction provision and use in public libraries, the low-key approach seems a curious anomaly. It could be argued that, for public librarians, fiction is the one area which demands comprehensive exploitation, much as information scientists exploit specialized subject areas for their own clienteles. Treatment of this kind would require public libraries to adopt a whole new approach, not to mention a new recruitment policy.

Management of fiction provision

Despite the scale of fiction provision in public libraries, few authorities exploit fiction stocks in the way suggested above. In fact a 1979 survey *The provision of fiction in 12 library authorities*[193] suggested that public libraries took the management of fiction provision a good deal less seriously than they do non-fiction. Few authorities had any central policy for the provision of fiction, or set up allocations for particular types of fiction, or offered librarians at service points any working brief which would assist in selection.

Selection decisions were often made without considering all available sources of information, speed and ease of supply being apparently deemed more important than finding out what was worth buying. Fiction reviews were rarely consulted – surprisingly, in view of their unique contribution to evaluating new novels (see below). Known authors were favoured to the disadvantage of new talents. It was rare to find an authority which made any arrangements to ensure comprehensive coverage of new fiction – although such arrangements were almost always made for non-fiction.

Equally, few authorities exercised any central monitoring of fiction weeding, to ensure that copies of important titles were retained in the authority. In Britain this is particularly unfortunate because the British Library – the country's main source of interlending – does not hold loan copies of fiction. Exceptionally, some authorities do maintain reserve stocks of older standard fiction, often in a fiction store, to which are sent all withdrawals judged likely to be useful. Some of these collections are considerable – from 10,000 to 20,000 volumes – and have their value enhanced by printed catalogues which publicize the contents.

The impression of unevenness in fiction provision is supported by some of the statistical information provided by the Registrar of Public Lending Right, which compares the variations in loans between 20 different libraries in the course of one year. Of the 315,528 titles stocked in total between the 20 libraries, 43% were held in only one library. Only 5% were held at 10 of the 20 libraries, whilst a mere 0.3% were held in all 20. It is true that these figures cover non-fiction as well as fiction titles, but fiction forms the bulk of these loans, and the extremely low number of common holdings between the 20 libraries is surprising and thought-provoking.

The evaluation of fiction

Because of its subjective nature, fiction tends to be difficult to evaluate. The comparison or ranking of individual authors is an invidious task. Originality cannot be measured, only recognized. Discussion of this subject is thrown into confusion by the question of taste. 'I know what I like', is unanswerable, if it is true. The idea that some measure of agreement can be reached about artistic merit (or entertainment value) in novels is by no means

157

generally accepted.

Nevertheless the librarian *must* choose. He has a professional responsibility to identify merit. Various methods have been suggested to achieve this identification. Of these, the notion that the librarian himself can 'review' novels personally is a controversial one. Library staff may not have the time to evaluate books in this fashion, nor be capable of the specialized skills that this requires. In fact the examination of 'on approval' copies of fiction by librarians is scarcely worthwhile at all unless (as with classic novels) there are several editions of the same title to compare or (as with light fiction) the 'sameness' of individual titles within the genre means that editions can be rejected because of small print size, poor production or some other factor not connected with the quality of the text. The factors which render perusal of non-fiction books by librarians a meaningful activity (clues to quality and content such as the preface, list of contents, bibliography, etc.) do not apply in a novel, where only a reading and evaluation of the text itself will serve. The librarian's function then is to discover what other sources of evaluation exist and to produce a synthesis of these which can be linked to his knowledge of the library's clientele.

Reputation of the publisher
A knowledge of publishers' specializations and reputations is useful in the selection of both fiction and non-fiction – perhaps less so for fiction where much of the output is from general publishing houses, whose lists have no outstanding characteristics one way or another. All the same, most publishers do 'shape' their fiction lists to some extent, and become known for quality (or lack of it) in a particular fiction genre.

Paperback imprints
The present structure of the book trade, where paperbacks appear about one year after publication of the hardback, means that hardbacks provide an ideal testing ground for market research on the potential of a paperback edition. Those titles which do appear in paperback may be judged to have succeeded in their line. For instance one might almost use the Penguin catalogue as a stock list of modern middlebrow quality fiction, and other paperback imprints can similarly be taken as standard lists of best-

selling authors. Librarians should make use of this approach with caution, precisely because of the need for the public library to balance out commercial pressures and to encourage lesser-known writers whose early novels do not reach paperback format.

Prizes

Receipt of a literary prize is a clear indication of consensus approval for a writer, either from his/her own profession or from literary or cultural institutions. Britain offers fewer prizes than most countries, but even so there remains a substantial number. The largest of these, the Booker Prize, has consistently rewarded original and under-publicized writers. A list of prizes, including those for various types of light fiction, appears annually in *Writers' and artists' yearbook*[313]

Press reviews

The major source of evaluative information about new novels is to be found in book reviews in daily and Sunday newspapers, and in the literary sections of certain weekly journals. A survey carried out in 1978[193] suggests that most 'serious' fiction *is* reviewed. Eighty-two per cent of serious fiction received at least one review in the main reviewing papers – established authors (89%) being better reviewed than the writers of first, second or third novels. 'Mysteries' also received good review coverage. On the other hand, review coverage of 'Westerns' and 'romances' was virtually non-existent, while coverage of 'historical romances' and 'family sagas' was sketchy. The survey also examined the delays occurring between publication of novels and publication of the reviews relating to them. For instance, within a period of two months after publication 85% of the reviews relating to 'serious' fiction and 74% of those relating to 'mysteries' had been published.

A 1987 survey of fiction reviews by Turner[308] reports similar findings. Sixty-eight per cent of 'literary fiction' was reviewed at least once, mostly in the two months following publication.

Few public librarians appear to make use of book reviews in their fiction selection on any planned basis. Most read some reviews from the newspapers which they happen to take in their homes, and draw upon this information from memory when considering fiction titles for selection at a book meeting or when examining 'on approval' copies. There is rarely any attempt to build up coverage by library staff of all the important book reviewing papers, or to note down the findings of staff review reading in any systematic fashion.

Various reasons have been put forward for not using reviews. It is claimed that newspaper reviews are aimed at the general public, and are therefore not useful for librarians; that the wide variations in different reviewers' appraisals also detract from their usefulness; that new fiction must be rushed on to library shelves as quickly as possible to make inroads into readers' waiting lists; or that late orders can result in titles being reported out-of-print.

Most of these objections are unrealistic. Newspaper reviews of novels offer at the very least a brief summary of plot and an evaluation of content which are scarcely less valuable to the librarian than to the layman. They provide virtually the only evaluation available for novels. Differences of view amongst different reviewers must be accepted as inevitable in such a controversial field, but a reading of disparate opinions is valuable in affording a more rounded picture of the novel.

Late orders for books can occasionally result in an out-of-print report, and this is certainly a risk of a carefully weighed decision. It is however unlikely to occur in the case of works by unknown novelists, where the publisher must usually struggle to sell out even a modest edition. A number of authors are so well known that their latest offerings will be heavily in demand whatever their critical reception. One common library treatment for such authors is a pre-publication order, although even for the most popular novelists this should be a cautious one, since a writer's work tends to vary in quality from title to title (though initial library demand does not vary much). In the case of new or lesser-known novelists a delay to take account of review opinions is nearly always the most effective approach.

Standard fiction lists
In programmes of fiction stock revision, some authorities rely heavily on the standard fiction lists produced by library suppliers. These are useful checklists, but an over-reliance on library suppliers leads to an over-emphasis on the standard and more saleable commodities and neglect of specialized interests. Library suppliers' lists contain the majority of important titles in print,

but by no means all. Stock revision conducted solely from these sources will tend to neglect titles which are only published in paperback or by unusual hardback publishers (including some of the classic novels), and also a range of important but lesser known modern authors whose work is not profitable enough for library suppliers to hold in stock. Library suppliers have no qualitative criteria for inclusion of a title on such lists: much of their content is ephemeral material for which the sole criterion for inclusion is saleability. In view of these limitations many library authorities now produce their own select lists of standard fiction authors.

The light fiction question

Librarians face a recurrent problem in developing and implementing a policy for fiction provision. It is extremely difficult to break down the large amounts of fiction purchased (in the way that the non-fiction sections can be broken down by the classification system), so that priorities can be attached to some types of material and not to others. Similarly, library users have trouble – as described above – finding their way in the single alphabetical sequence comprising thousands of books. Over the years there have been several attempts to classify the contents of novels (Pejterson's article[190] gives a good summary of the literature), but none have had any practical success.

Classification of fiction by form is more common. A binary division is often made, into 'serious' or 'literary' on the one hand, and 'light', 'recreational' or 'genre' on the other. This is not entirely satisfactory (some titles do not fit comfortably into any preconceived category) but nevertheless has a fair measure of acceptance among librarians and public alike. As to what constitutes a 'serious' rather than a 'light' work of fiction, Peter Mann's reference[285] to writing which *challenges* (rather than reinforces) the reader's attitudes and beliefs is probably as good as any. The same point was pursued in Q. D. Leavis's *Fiction and the reading public*,[183] a ferocious denunciation of the trivialization of reading tastes in Britain since the nineteenth century.

'Serious' fiction can be broken down a little further, into categories such as 'short stories' or 'classics' or even 'modern classics'. Beyond this one is hard put to suggest any further meaningful subdivisions, and the reader is still faced with a

161

considerable, undigestible mass of works, for which only a subdivision by author is likely (and then only for cognoscenti) to give clues to style or content.

Most 'light' fiction can, of course, be further broken down into the various genres, though not all librarians are in favour of doing so. Dixon, discussing genre fiction in great detail, is one who argues against dividing by genre. Nevertheless, publishers commonly package their fiction so that the genre is instantly recognizable, whilst a majority of readers pursue particular genres, so libraries are probably right to employ – as many do – a genre classification on their shelves.

There seems to be no good reason for public librarians to become embroiled in discussions on the merits of recreational reading. There are very strong arguments for providing a generous measure of good light fiction in all public libraries. The demand for this material is heavier than for any other, and most public library users, whatever their regular reading tastes, require access to light fiction at one time or another. Libraries are financed through local government taxes, to which all members of the community contribute, thus warranting representation for all tastes. At one level, light fiction is concerned with sustaining literacy (although a majority of romance and mystery readers in fact come from the literate middle classes).

Nor should it be suggested that part of a librarian's function is to proselytize, nudging readers towards 'a better kind of novel'. Users may justifiably regard this philosophy as inappropriate and patronizing. The librarian's job is to *make available* a cross-section of all kinds of fiction, and to provide users with every available means for exploiting the collection.

The key question is not whether public libraries should provide light fiction, but what proportions should be provided in relation to serious fiction. Should provision merely echo use, with 80% of fiction funding going to light fiction? Should it simply reflect the quantitative patterns of publishing, which again would result in a heavy preponderance of light *vis-à-vis* serious reading?

There is no 'right' answer to this, and no scientific formula for allocating fiction funding. It is an area where librarians must make value judgements. My own view, bearing in mind Mann's comment about 'challenging readers' attitudes and beliefs', is that a heavy weighting in favour of serious fiction provision is justified.

The element of 'sameness' in much of the genre fiction is likely to provide its readers with a much higher level of acceptable substitutability between titles. Whereas 'serious' fiction, with its genuine (if often flawed) attempt at originality, is less amenable to substitution by other titles.

In practice this might mean, for instance, that at least one title of all serious new fiction should be put into stock, while genre novels that were deemed 'bad of their kind' would not be ordered at all. Only by providing practical guidelines of this kind can librarians ensure that their authority actually has a fiction policy. What is required is a definition of the various types of fiction to be supplied, a clear statement of priorities between them (backed up by appropriate allocations), and a monitoring of subsequent expenditure.

Summary

In quantitative terms fiction has long been the public library's most important service, and yet it is rarely taken seriously. Whatley's 1956 article[197] pleading for a more imaginative approach, was ahead of its time, but that time has come and gone without perceptible improvement in services. Subsequent articles by McClellan[185] and Olle[189] also argued powerfully for serious treatment of the form. The appearance of recent studies – particularly those by Goodall and by Sear and Jennings – is helpful, but practical measures are also required from library authorities. The message of recent literature is clear. There is a need for fiction to be carefully selected and then *exploited*, for a public which makes intensive use of the service, but patently needs expert advice. This is a major opportunity, since public libraries are the obvious agencies to provide assistance.

As things stand, public libraries play an important role in fiction publishing, virtually carrying the hardback editions of first and second novels, whose imprints only run to 800 or so copies. Normally there is no reason why libraries should sustain speculative publishing ventures, but the position of fiction is a very special one, with a majority of public library users relying heavily on the long lists of novels turned out by 'standard' fiction authors. Obviously, an author who does not publish a first or second novel will not publish a ninth or tenth either, and the least that librarians can do is to consider the output of new novels carefully and purchase those which are well reviewed. In playing a positive role in support of new novels, librarians can also contribute to the survival of the public library's most important source of raw material.

21 *Biography*

'Biographies' in public libraries constitute one of the most important and best used sections of the stock, and their provision raises several interesting points which are valid for other areas of non-fiction. Asked, in the 1988 Euromonitor surveys,[130] what type of book they were reading at the time of the survey, 8% of the respondents replied 'biography'. Although this answer fell a long way behind the most common reply – fiction, at 69% – it came ahead of all other categories (history 6%, education 3%, religion 3%, etc.). Similarly, Luckham's 1971 survey of library use[60] showed 10% of users borrowing biography, compared with 72% fiction, 10% geography and travel, and 5% history. The figures are not unalike, and it seems clear that amongst people who read for pleasure, biography comes second only to fiction as a source of reading material. One may take 'biography' to include related forms such as autobiography, diaries and letters, and the definition could well be expanded to include travel books, since these are often autobiographical in approach.

An obvious problem of provision is that biography serves a dual purpose. At one extreme, a biography may be a scholarly work of history aimed at researchers interested in a particular period or subject area. At the other may be found many trivialized records of the lives of show-biz personalities – works intended entirely for recreational reading. Midway between these two poles is a rapidly increasing body of biographical work which may be read purposively or for pleasure, or both, and it is with these that librarians ordering books for public libraries must largely be concerned.

Most public libraries receive some explicit demand for this material – usually just after its publication, often proportionate to the fame of the biographee, and often hard to resist. But as the numbers of published biographies increase (to an extent that was unimaginable 20 years ago) librarians must seek the sort of indicators of lasting quality which distinguish 'standard' fiction authors in bibliographies and select lists. Lord Quinton, in a stirring speech – later an article[201] – recently referred to 'the best that has been thought and said', and went on: 'The most serious threat to culture at the present moment is the assault against the idea that there is any canon at all, any objectively definable elite of books which should be addressed to in preference to others . . . .'

Notwithstanding difficulties of identification, there clearly is a core or 'canon' of biographical work which for one reason or another has established a foothold in the permanent literature, and which recurs with surprising frequency in discussion of the form. It enlarges by accretion, since biographical literature does not date to any extent. In fact an increasing number of older works are being restored to print in response to a recent surge of public interest in the genre.

Little has been written on the use of biography in libraries, though Spiller's article[202] attempts to suggest features which might be used to identify biographies of genuine and lasting quality. Amongst these he explores the objectivity of the biographer (or 'honesty' in the case of an autobiographer), the occupation and celebrity of the subject, the originality of treatment, and the extent to which biography successfully amalgamates the private and public lives of the biographee.

Finally, biography provision highlights the problem created by library classification systems *via-à-vis* users' needs to browse for general reading. Most libraries now follow BNB/MARC practice of classifying biography with subject, so that user choice from the shelves is demarcated by the biographee's occupation. Whilst there are often strong reasons for taking this line – politicians, for instance, are difficult to separate from the history of their period – the fact remains that many users enter their public libraries looking for 'a biography', and the splintering of the former 'biography sections' into hundreds of different shelf locations is not helpful.

McClellan long ago observed, in a key paper,[200] that public libraries tend to be organized around the purposive readers, and that readers for whom browsing is the principal form of approach may actually find the classification system a barrier. He devised an alternative way of displaying stock to mitigate the problem. McClellan's model layout of a library, arranged for what he called 'service in depth', had an area for 'diversionary' literature (containing browsable non-fiction) located immediately beyond the entrance, with purposive reading areas situated beyond these.

In the past few years, ideas along these lines have been developed in a number of public library authorities. A book by Ainley and Totterdell [199] describes several of the experiments – all concerned with breaking away from traditional Dewey arrangements to present library stock in ways felt to be more appropriate to user needs. The term 'stock categorization' is often used to describe such new arrangements. It is hard to see that the process of breaking up classified sequences can go very far beyond McClellan's original conception of a 'diversionary literature' section, while the library's information function is also retained. However, some of the recent experiments do go considerably further. The success of any new arrangements of this kind will depend very much upon mutual cooperation between selector and cataloguer, and indeed some of the authorities experimenting in this way arrange for the two processes to be carried out by the same staff.

22 *Audiovisual materials*

This chapter considers the provision of recorded sound (records, cassettes and compact discs), films and videos, still visuals, microforms and computer software. Audiovisual (AV) provision demands some differences in approach from the provision of print materials, but there are differences too in the treatment required for each individual medium. Generalizations are rarely valid, and provision must be based upon an approach worked out separately for each type of material.

Discussion of provision must also be related to type of library. AV provision is most fully developed in school libraries, which are outside the scope of this book, but provision has also been greatly extended in academic and public libraries in the past 15 years. The latter have long been involved in the provision of gramophone records and cassettes, and microforms. The past few years have seen the introduction of compact discs, and in some authorities, videos and computer software.

In academic libraries, provision tends to vary according to the status of the institution. University libraries have very substantial collections of microforms, but the polytechnics and colleges are generally much more committed to large collections of other media. A 1983 survey by Heery[208] of 210 'degree-awarding institutions' showed that polytechnics and colleges held really substantial collections of audio recordings, slides and illustrations, and moderately large collections of videos. A later (1988) survey of AV provision in the higher education sector by Thompson[305] reported that 22 institutions (nearly all universities) held 'mostly print' collections, whilst 52, comprising polytechnics, colleges of higher education and universities, were multimedia.

Many academic institutions have audiovisual departments which *produce* material. These may be jointly managed with the library, linked, or entirely separate.

The major holdings of AV materials are in very large special collections, such as the British Film Institute, the various BBC libraries, and the National Sound Archive (formerly the British Institute of Recorded Sound). These collections are very sizeable indeed, and have developed their own systems of selection and organization to a point where generalized descriptions here would have little value. But for any librarian involved in AV provision, a knowledge of the major collections is essential.

Amongst librarians in recent years, enthusiasm for non-book materials as such has sometimes overshadowed the need to identify the relative contributions to be made, in terms of content, by each of the media *vis-à-vis* the more traditional forms of printed word materials. Comparative costs are an important factor. Although the price of a compact disc, slide, microform, etc., is comparable with the price of an average non-fiction book, the cost of purchase and maintenance of the audiovisual hardware is a large additional expenditure which tends to be overlooked. Many librarians therefore find themselves in the position of having to justify to their financing authorities the expansion of their collection to include one of the new media. Outside the field of school resource centres there are few standards for non-book materials provision which librarians can turn to to support their case. The American Library Association's *Guidelines for audio-visual materials and services for large public libraries*,[203] published in 1975, recommends that 10% – 15% of the budget of a large public library should be allocated to non-book materials, a recommendation described in the *Audiovisual librarian* review,[239] as having a 'slightly unreal air'. More to the point, perhaps, is that librarians should think out the relevance of each medium for particular purposes, so that the kind of question asked is 'Is this a more effective form than the printed word?' or even – when there are severe financial constraints – 'Is this medium the only way of putting over a certain concept or is there another, cheaper medium available?'

Shortage of material

In the case of some of the media, intensive production is a relatively recent phenomenon, and for others production is always likely to remain at a relatively modest level. Searching for material on a subject basis can be a frustrating task for there is often nothing suitable published (produced), even where the subject lends itself to treatment by a particular medium. The situation may be contrasted with that of the printed word, where it is rare to draw a complete blank in a subject search. The tendency for audiovisual material to date rapidly contributes to the dearth of material. In short, there is often no 'selection' to be made – a fact which in universities frequently leads to the internal production of audiovisual materials. It can also happen that there is a dearth of materials to fit certain pieces of equipment. As a rule, hardware should not be purchased until a full range of appropriate software is known to be available.

Bibliographical control

Though patchy, bibliographical control of AV materials in Britain is a good deal better than it was. The British Library Act of 1972[250] provides a legislative basis for action by referring to a 'comprehensive collection of books, manuscripts, periodicals, films and other recorded material, whether printed or otherwise', and the British Library's recent involvement in the bibliography of AV materials has greatly improved the situation – see their 'public statement' in 1983[206] and Pinion's report on legal deposit.[210] Two other important institutions are the British Universities Film and Video Council (BUF&VC) and the Educational Foundation for Visual Aids (EFVA). The chapter on acquisition in Fothergill and Butchart's *Non-book materials in libraries*[207] contains a good, though slightly out-of-date summary of the bibliographical control situation, and other recent articles are helpful.[205, 209] A summary of the problems is attempted below, and some examples of useful bibliographies are given.

A knowledge of what is easily available and obtainable is the AV user's main concern, since the bibliographical and interlending resources enjoyed by book users have traditionally been lacking. Two approaches are common – 'in print' listings and catalogues of large collections.

Amongst notable 'in print' listings are the *Gramophone* catalogues of recorded sound, and the *Guide to microforms in print*. The invaluable BUF&VC's *Higher education learning programmes information services catalogue* (HELPIS) lists films, videos, sound recordings and slide sets which are intended for use in institutions of higher education and are available for purchase or hire.

HELPIS is a database, updated monthly, issued in an annual volume or on microfiche, and accessible through the BLAISE-LINE online bibliographic service. In addition to general sources of this kind, publishers' catalogues play a particularly important role in establishing the availability of AV materials.

The prime example of a large collection, available for hire or purchase, is that of the Educational Foundation for Visual Aids.

Selective, evaluative listings of AV materials are still the exception rather than the rule, though two outstanding examples are the Penguin *Guide to compact discs, cassettes and LP's*, which compares all available recordings of classical music, and Maltin's annual *TV movies and video guide*, which gives reliable brief reviews of all feature films which have appeared.

Review coverage of new AV materials is still relatively poor (with the notable exception of the *Gramophone* journal's reviews of music), and AV librarians need to hunt around to discover useful sources for their particular media.

Whilst collections of printed media are built up against a background of national cooperative schemes for interlending and photocopying, AV collections normally have to aim at independent provision, because of the scarcity of interlending facilities. The British Library Document Supply Centre does not handle AV materials, and the Greater London Audio Specialisation Scheme (GLASS) for the interlending of discs and tapes is a rare example of its kind.

Previewing of audiovisual materials

There are some benefits for librarians in previewing AV materials before selection, though the advantages of doing so are probably overrated. Information on the content and level of each item and on its suitability for user groups – the kind of information obtained, in the case of a book, by leafing through the introduction and contents page – can usually be obtained for AV materials from the bibliographical record or from the description in the publisher's catalogue. Bibliographical descriptions for AV materials are generally fuller than for printed word materials. The BUF&VC lists, for instance, now include annotations.

The main advantage of previewing lies in the evaluation of technical qualities. Considerations of visual quality, sound reproduction, suitability for machinery, variations of format, etc.

171

are generally more important than consideration of the corresponding physical factors in book selection (though still subordinate to the content of the item concerned).

However there are practical difficulties which restrict pre-purchase access to AV materials. Illegal copying is a simple operation for many of the media, and manufacturers are unlikely to yield to entreaties for approval copies. In view of this, some librarians pay periodic visits to one of the large collections of AV materials, where they can at one and the same time find out what is available and examine items of interest. The Audio Visual Reference Centre of the BUF&VC, and the Scottish Council for Educational Technology, offer facilities of this kind. Also, some library suppliers have taken AV provision seriously, and are useful sources of information about new productions.

Weeding of audiovisual materials

The criteria for withdrawing AV materials from stock are much the same as for books – that is to say, because the content is out-of-date, or the physical condition is unsatisfactory, or the items are not being used. Where physical condition is concerned, most of the non-book media wear out very much faster than print on a page, and few libraries aim at the semi-archival collections typical of the printed word, where important or 'classic' works in the field are retained indefinitely as an essential part of the total stock. To some extent this throws additional emphasis upon the need for subject coverage.

Sound recordings

Collections of recorded sound based upon gramophone records and audio cassettes have been an important component of public library services for many years. Building up these collections has been both facilitated and complicated since 1983 by the appearance of the compact disc. Librarians must now select between three different formats which offer different musical repertoires at different prices. User preferences remain the most important factor in deciding between these three, but selectors must also attempt to look into the future and decide which formats will flourish indefinitely, and which might be more short-lived.

Undoubtedly the compact disc's durability and high quality sound give it great advantages over records and cassettes as a medium for library use. Though prices are currently 30% – 40% higher than for the other two media, they ultimately offer increased value for money, and many public libraries have already developed substantial collections.

Gramophone records and audio cassettes have competed for library business for over a decade. In terms of recording quality, cassettes have now improved to a point of parity or near parity with records, so that sound quality is really not a factor that need concern public librarians in general (although of course the quality of individual recordings may vary from record to cassette). In terms of physical durability cassettes certainly have the edge, often giving five or six years service and up to 100 issues, compared with the more rapid wear upon records. Experts are predicting the demise of the long-playing record by the end of the century (though traditional media often prove surprisingly resistant to expert predictions).

There are distinct variations in coverage between the three media. Recordings may appear on two or three formats, or uniquely on one (already, a number of recordings are appearing on compact disc alone), and any collection aiming to be comprehensive must, for the time being, stock all three media. As Saddington and Cooper showed in their invaluable *Audio cassettes as library materials*,[213] the cassette's coverage of classical music has improved greatly over the past 10 years, and almost as many UK public libraries now stock cassettes as they do records. Spoken word recordings are also largely the preserve of the cassette medium.

Another policy decision to be made by selectors of sound recordings is whether to pursue the best recordings available, regardless of cost, or to concentrate on selecting from the many cheap labels on the market, so that a larger total stock can be acquired. The *Gramophone* reviews often compare bargains with expensive recordings of the same items.

Selection of classical music is characterized by one unusual feature, compared with the selection of books or many other materials. The *content* of collections is fairly stable, comprising the basic and well-known classical repertoire, augmented relatively rarely by new music, or revivals of old favourites. The evaluation process therefore concentrates principally upon performance of pieces rather than on the music content itself. To some extent this means that efforts are concentrated upon achieving an ideal balance within the traditional repertoire, as earlier additions to stock wear out, and new performances replace old ones.

Because of the existence of the *Gramophone* and other good reviewing journals, review coverage of music – particularly the classical repertoire – is almost comprehensive for British recordings. Reviews cover both performance and technical aspects, and are published soon enough for selection decisions to be based upon their appearance. For popular music and jazz the basic reviewing sources are supplemented by specialized journals such as *Melody maker*. A number of excellent selective guides to jazz and classical music have also appeared. The *Gramophone's* quarterly 'in print' catalogues ensure that information on availability is always on hand, and in any case efficient specialist suppliers of sound recordings can be found in most cities. Selectors of sound recordings in libraries are usually specialists.

Films

This section is chiefly concerned with 16mm (non-theatrical) film. A crucial factor about film is its high cost, which puts it beyond the budget of many libraries, and in fact Heery's survey[208] shows there are only very small film collections in most of the academic institutions surveyed. Film provision therefore falls mainly into two approaches: selection for a few large libraries which deal only in films, or selection of titles for borrowing by various types of educational institutions.

Harrison's chapter on film selection[221] lists various categories of special library – national, distribution, documentary production, feature production, government, governmental research, national archival, newsreel, television, educational – each with different objectives and different selection procedures. It is not possible to generalize on the approach to selection. However, Harrison isolates four important selection criteria which she considers apply to all types of library:

1. technical quality of the film;
2. its subject relevance to the existing collection;
3. cost;
4. copyright restrictions, and their effect upon use.

She considers the first two of these criteria to be the primary considerations.

Technical quality is clearly a very important factor (bearing in mind that many film libraries buy up supplies of secondhand film), and film stock should be avoided if fogged, out of focus, scratched, or showing signs of rapid deterioration. Nevertheless, if unique material is only available on poor film the librarian may still opt for selection.

The film's *content* and its relevance to other items in the collection are the primary considerations for selection. Educational institutions are rarely able to build a 'balanced' stock of films, provision being based upon response to individual projects. (This is true of most educational resource provision.) A good knowledge of other film collections is essential, so that the library's own stock can be supplemented by borrowing from outside sources.

Video

The relatively low price of video (considerably cheaper than film) brings it within the purchasing range of libraries of various kinds. Heery's survey[208] showed academic libraries having moderate collections of videos, many of these deriving from the production departments of their own or other academic institutions. Pinion's survey of *Video home lending services in public libraries*[216] showed that 25 out of 160 public library authorities surveyed had video lending services, very largely offering feature films.

The video boom in the world at large is dominated at present by entertainment videos, themselves monopolized by a few large communications conglomerates who supply everyone – high street vendors and libraries alike – with essentially the same stock. The main decisions faced by public librarians about video selection will be concerned with the kind of provision to be made, and the purpose of making it. Nearly half of the public libraries presently lending feature videos are doing so, in part at least, to raise income. Udwin points out[217] the tenuousness of this proposition, since high street vendors offering the same kind of stock have lower overheads and can therefore offer more competitive prices. He urges public libraries to move into other video areas more compatible with public library objectives – home recordings of local activities, loan copies of educational television programmes (if copyright restrictions were to be lifted), and the whole area of educational videos, of the kind produced by the Open University, the Arts Council, and firms such as Drake Educational Associates. However the Pinion survey showed that educational videos do not at present issue at all well. The whole matter clearly needs a great deal of thought.

Another decision to be made concerns format. There are a variety of incompatible formats available – cassettes, cartridges, disks, and a variety of systems within these. The VHS cassette format has had a profound effect upon libraries since its inception in 1978, and was shown by Pinion to be the most widely used system (followed by Betamax and Philips V2000).

Still visuals
The term 'still visuals' refers here to photographs, art reproductions, slides and filmstrips. Specialized collections of still visuals fall into one of four groups: national, private, commercial, educational. However, most types of library include some still visuals in their stock. Advice on the selection of these materials is to be found in the references to Shaw,[223] Pacey,[222] Harrison,[221] and Evans.[220]

The Arts Libraries Society (ARLIS) has made an impact in this area of work. It is much involved in stimulating research, and publishes the *Arts libraries journal* and a directory of collections.

In selecting art reproductions, the librarian's central concern is to achieve a high degree of faithfulness to the original. Absolute fidelity cannot be managed – as anyone who has compared an original with a reproduction will know. Colour quality is the chief problem, and here filmstrips and slides usually achieve a better result than printed reproductions – although they also tend to fade a few years after acquisition. Quality, in both transparent and printed reproductions, varies enormously. Librarians need to build up profiles of the main producers, and if possible (it usually *is* possible) to obtain examples on approval before purchase. The bibliography of the subject is scattered amongst various institutional and publishers' lists: there is no comprehensive listing.

The selection of photographs (of whatever subject) requires a rather different approach. Such is the quantity of material available that librarians need to be very careful to keep their collections within practical bounds. Shaw notes 'Intelligent picture selection implies a clear understanding of one's own collection and its gaps and a firm determination to exclude irrelevant or unsuitable pictures'. Even 'universal' collections should only include a manageable assortment of pictures in any one category. Obviously the boundaries are set by the type of collection – scientific, technical, educational, cultural, recreational or artistic – and the institutions' objectives. Public library collections are usually concerned with *local* objects and events.

The process of picture acquisition is different from that of most other materials since, typically, single pictures are purchased through an agency. A knowledge of agencies is therefore most important. Evans's *Picture researcher's handbook*[219] is an essential tool. Pictures may be acquired from commercial agencies, museums, galleries, print collectors, print shops, antique dealers, postal dealers and auctions and sales. They may also be commissioned from photographic dealers and agencies, or extracted from printed publications. Exchange programmes are often possible. If pictures are acquired through a gift, as many are, the librarian should insist on the right to select from those offered, and not, necessarily, to take the collection in its entirety.

Microforms

The assertion that each of the non-book media should be regarded as a form of communication in its own right only applies, in the case of microforms, up to a point. Microform is a medium involving words, and has traditionally been seen as a format which is complementary to the printed word. And since few users *like* microform for its own sake, selection of the medium must be geared to materials in which the advantages of the microformat outweigh user resistance to it. Teague[226] isolates three basic areas where microforms offer clear advantages:

1. areas of information provision which are not economic for the book (for instance, the publishing of very small editions);
2. instances when time and money can be saved by the use of microform (for instance, where microform copies of foreign reports are airmailed for user requests);
3. provision in libraries with acute space shortage problems.

The first of these areas is the one in which microform publishing is flourishing. With the economic margins of conventional

177

publishing shrinking, and worthwhile monographs and research results unable to find publishers, the microform publisher comes into his own. Typically, quantities of six up to 50 copies are all that is needed to make publication viable. The number and subject range of microforms available is growing. Ashby's book[224] gives many useful insights into the way microform publishers find their markets.

Two specific types of microform may be identified in this area. Firstly, the 'user propogated' work issues originally in print, and is then reissued in microform in response to limited user demand (this includes rare books). Secondly, works are planned and put out by the publisher as original microforms. There have been a number of recent, ambitious microform projects in both categories.

As may be judged from the outline of microform markets given above, the largest collections of microforms are to be found in academic and national libraries. All the same, it would be rare to find a library, of any type, which does not contain some microforms, and the medium has so far shown considerable resilience in resisting the threat of online and CD-ROM services, which operate in many of the microform's natural markets.

Librarians sometimes need to choose between printed and microformed versions of the same text – or choose to take both. Some journals are available in both forms, and some American university presses publish the two versions of works simultaneously. Other examples are newspaper files (usually held in microform for back issues rather than current ones), telephone directories, government publications, reference works, and bibliographies – particularly when frequently updated.

A decision between the various microformats is rarely required, since most micro-titles are offered in one format only. However, Teague's book includes recommendations for the types of literature he considers most suitable for each format.

Decisions on the selection of microform titles can be exceptionally difficult, since many microform publishers concentrate on the publication of very large series, where singling out of titles within the series is invidious, yet purchase of the entire collection inordinately expensive.

A great deal is written on technical aspects of micro-publishing, but bibliographical control is less fully treated. The conventional bibliographical tools cannot be relied upon for this medium, and recourse must be had to separate microform bibliographies – particularly 'in print' listings, and individual publishers' catalogues.

Computer software

Computer software can be divided into three types:

1. applications software (e.g. for accounting), with library use largely limited to special libraries in the subject;
2. computer assisted learning, for which the main library demand will be felt, especially in education institutions;
3. hobbies and games – largely for home consumption, though with some possible public library applications, e.g. chess, language learning.

Software collections for libraries are still in their early stages, and the main selection problem faced is trying to trace what is available. Tage's report[231] describes the difficulties, notably a very irregular distribution pattern through publishers, local specialist distributors, bookshops, education projects and many other sources. There are various types of software publisher – book publishers, computer manufacturers, specialist suppliers – and they vary tremendously in size. Despite the very rapid increase in the amount of software available, there is no real bibliographical control as yet, and selectors must have recourse to trade literature, periodicals and advertisements in computer journals. Public library stocks of software are often borrowed (rather than purchased) from software companies, despite running disputes over copyright problems.

Where material is used in-house, the librarian's choice is obviously restricted to what is compatible with the machines owned. Public library loan collections can range more widely over different formats.

Some recent literature on the subject has appeared. Fielden[229] listed a number of technical criteria for the selection of software, amongst which the most important were considered to be the reputation of the manufacturer, the user friendliness of the system, and the quality of the manual. Ebrahim[228] described the Bedford micro project, in which home and business microcomputers were made available in Bedfordshire public libraries for use by members. Skinner[230] described the results of a survey carried out in 1984 – 6, finding that out of 156 public library authorities surveyed, 33 lent microcomputer software to the public, 50 were considering it in the near future, and 47 had considered it, but rejected the idea – usually because they could not afford the initial stock. The reasons for offering this service were usually a mixture of satisfying demand and needing to raise income through charging for the service. £1,000 was reckoned to be the average cost of purchasing the initial stock. A typical picture, in the libraries surveyed, was one of heavy demand and insufficient stock.

23 Databases

The use of databases, accessed through telecommunications links and searched online, is an information retrieval technique which has become familiar to most librarians over the past decade. In 1989 it was estimated that some 2,000 online databases were available. These are sometimes classified into 'referral' databases (containing bibliographic citations or reference material), numerical databases, and full-text databases (containing major works such as the *Oxford English dictionary* or the complete works of Shakespeare). A considerable bibliography already exists – including *On-line bibliographical databases* by J. L. Hall and M. J. Brown (Aslib, 3rd ed. 1983), an excellent example of a selective bibliography in its field.

A more recent information retrieval medium is the invaluable CD-ROM (Compact Disc – Read Only Memory). Information is contained on a purchased or leased disc (identical in form to the recorded sound compact disc), and searched in-house on a pc/disc drive combination – so that no additional charges are incurred once the original disc has been acquired. Despite the fairly recent arrival of this medium on the information scene, at least one substantial bibliography – *CD-ROM directory 1989* (published by TFPL) – has already been issued.

To write of 'selection' procedures for databases may strike a quaint note, but the development of CD-ROMs – which are *acquired* in much the same way as books or periodicals – underlines the fact that the use of databases must be preceded by selection decisions, which lead to the commitment of money. The decisions relate to which databases will be used for a particular subject area, but also to whether the information will be paid for online, or through the purchase of CD-ROMs, or through purchase of the original print copy (which in many instances runs

181

parallel with an automated version), or by subscribing to one of the automated versions *and* the print version of the same item.

From a growing literature, the following are recommended for advice on selection. Grogan's work,[263] though now out-of-date, gives a detailed and clear description of the way that databases operate. Foster's *Which data base?*,[233] though concentrating on information sources in business and the social sciences, and written in 1981, gives a number of pointers to evaluating databases and their suppliers which are of application in all subject fields. Houghton and Wisdom[234] discuss non-bibliographic online databases in economics and business studies subjects (largely falling into the category of 'numerical' database). Royce[236] covers recent developments in CD-ROM databases. Large[235] compares the use of online and CD-ROM reference sources. Whilst Clarke[232] reviews the parallel publishing of print and automated versions of information sources.

Before we try to evaluate and compare the sources of information themselves, a word should be said on the middlemen (the service suppliers or system operators) who afford access to online databases on an international scale, over a variety of telecommunications links. In effect the service suppliers use their own computers to repackage data for users. The qualities of databases and their service suppliers are therefore inextricably linked, and the evaluation process must extend to the latter.

Foster, amongst other commentators, suggests criteria for the evaluation of service suppliers.

1. The number and range of databases offered.
2. The number of search languages offered, and the simplicity of the search software – in particular, whether it is 'command' or 'menu' driven.
3. The availability of special search devices – e.g. truncation of search terms.
4. The system's performance (i.e. speed of response).
5. The print formats available.
6. Accessibility of the service, in terms of opening hours.
7. The customer support offered.
8. Costs and charging policy, including the cost of training, the signing-on fee, and the way that charges are made (for instance, on search time or results).

Evaluation of the databases themselves can be a complex process. Not only must databases be compared against others in the same subject area, but where they exist in both online and CD-ROM modes, the two formats must be compared for effectiveness (and further compared against any print versions which are also in existence).

Amongst important criteria for evaluation of referral databases are:

1. The subject coverage of one database in relation to others. This is not always straightforward, since for effective results (particularly in the social sciences) more than one database will often need to be searched, and the right *combination* must therefore be selected. Cost-effective choices can only be made on the advice of staff who are experienced in searching a number of different tools.

2. Sources covered, such as the types of literature included (books, journals, reports, etc.), and whether foreign language materials are included. Also, the tool's comprehensiveness, within its stated limits. Retrospective coverage may differ between online and ROM services, especially in the humanities.

3. Currency – i.e. delays between publication of the documents cited, and their addition to the database. There is a wide variety of practice, and some delays are very lengthy indeed. The consumer will not know the true position, unless some research has been carried out by an independent body.

4. Effectiveness of the indexing and retrieval systems used.

5. Support system, including documentation, and the existence (or otherwise) of a help desk.

6. Costs. Most online searches comprise four cost elements: data producer's charge; service supplier's charge; telecommunications charge; (optional) print-out charge. These costs, when cumulated, mean that online searching adds a considerable and frequently recurring expense to a library's budget. By comparison, CD-ROM costs are all in the original purchase. Once a library has purchased a CD-ROM database, cost effectiveness increases with increasing use. On the other hand, original purchase costs of CD-ROMs are high. An average annual subscription to a bibliographical database on ROM is likely to be in the region of £500 – £1,000. Librarians need to estimate in advance the likely

amount of use of a database, before deciding whether to purchase the ROM or obtain access through online services. A user requiring access to a large number of different databases is likely to find online more cost effective than ROM. The costs of equipment for both systems are another factor.

Some additional factors are relevant for numerical databases. Their numbers are increasing rapidly (already outstripping referral databases), and their use is likely to become an increasingly important feature of work in specialized libraries in the areas of economics and business studies. The single most important feature of such databases is likely to be the facility which is offered for data computation or analysis – such as correlation, regression analysis and model building – and effective software analysis tools are essential if the full potential of the databases is to be realized. Many of the existing products are American, and the degree of American bias in content is therefore a factor for European users.

Clarke's valuable article[232] compares electronic databases with print versions of the same. The comparative cost benefits are heavily loaded in favour of print, although for a very expensive print item (e.g. the Kirk-Othmer *Encyclopaedia of chemical technology*) a very large number of searches could be run up before the cost of the print version was reached. Print is easier to use, and can be *browsed* – often a crucial advantage. Electronic media score heavily when currency is important (as long as they are properly kept up-to-date). However, as Clarke observes, electronic databases often omit some material which appears in the print versions, notably introductory matter, and any tables or figures in the text. For certain information sources this is a big disadvantage, and is something to be checked out before purchase. Clarke concludes that no generalized guidelines on selection can be valid. Each individual decision must be made on the basis of trading off several factors against the specific requirement.

Further reading

General works on book provision

1   Ayres, F. H., 'Stock provision' in *British librarianship and information work 1976 – 80*, Library Association, 1983. Literature review of the period.
2   Ayres, F. H., 'Stock provision' in *British librarianship and information work 1981 – 85 Vol. 2*, Library Association, 1988, 156 – 66. Literature review of the period.
3   Booth, P., 'Selection and acquisition: books and periodicals' in Anthony, L. J., *Handbook of special librarianship and information work*, Aslib, 5th ed., 1982.
4   Buckland, M. K., 'The roles of collections and the scope of collection development', *Journal of documentation*, **45** (3), Sept. 1989, 213 – 26. Attempt to place collection development within a conceptual framework.
5   Corrall, S., *Collection development: options for effective management*, Proceedings of a conference of the Library and Information Research Group, Univ. of Sheffield, 1987, Taylor Graham, 1988. Contributions on all types of library. Note especially the following: Bloomfield, B., 'Collection development: the key issues', 3–15; Heaney, H., 'The university research library', 17 – 27; Castens, M., 'The polytechnic library', 28 – 45; Ford, G., 'A review of relegation practice', 71–87; Horwill, C., 'Periodicals reviewing by voting', 102 –10; Woodward, H., 'Journal acquisition versus article acquisition', 111–17.
6   Curley, A. and Broderick, D., *Building library collections*. (Formerly by Carter and Bonk). Scarecrow Press, 6th ed., 1985. Strong emphasis on bibliography throughout.
7   Line, M., 'Can book selection be improved?' (Review essay), *British journal of academic librarianship*, **1** (2), Summer 1986, 160 – 6.

8 Ranganathan, S. R., *Library book selection*, Asia Publishing House, 2nd ed., 1966.

9 Stewart, L., *Public library research: a review of UK investigation between 1978 and 1982*, Centre for Library and Information Management, University of Loughborough, 1984. Pages 22 – 34 on materials.

10 Thompson, J. and Carr, R., *An introduction to university library administration*, Bingley, 4th ed., 1987. Pages 74 – 119 on collections.

11 Winkworth, L., 'Stock management and disposal: collection building and demolition' in Line, M. B., *Academic library management*, Library Association, 1990, 51 – 63.

Chapter 3   Policy

12 Apted, S., *Information materials policy statements in libraries in England and Wales*, Dept. of Librarianship, City of Birmingham Polytechnic, 1977. Results of this project summarized in the author's article in *New library world*, **79** (37), July 1978, 126 – 8.

13 Capital Planning Information, *Trends in public library selection policies*, BNB Research Fund, 1987.

14 Cronin, B., 'The uncontested orthodoxy', *British journal of academic librarianship*, **3** (1), Spring 1988, 1 – 8.

15 Enright, B. J., 'Concepts of stock: comprehensive vs. selective', in Line, M. B., *Academic library management*, Library Association, 1990, 36 – 50.

16 Futas, E., *Library acquisition policies and procedures*, Oryx Press, 1977. Examples of policy statements, all from American public and academic libraries.

17 Gore, D., 'Farewell to Alexandria: the theory of the no-growth, high-performance library', in Gore, D. (ed.), *Farewell to Alexandria: solutions to space, growth and performance problems of libraries*, Greenwood Press, 1976, 164 – 80.

18 Heeks, P. and Turner, P. (eds.), *Public library aims and objectives*, Public Libraries Research Group, 1981.

19 Hoare, P. A., 'Loads of learned lumber: special collections in the smaller university library', in Dyson, B. (ed.), *The modern academic library: essays in memory of Philip Larkin*, Library Association, 1989, 57 – 66.

20 McClellan, A. W., *The reader, the library and the book: selected papers 1949 – 70*, Bingley, 1973. Fundamental contributions to discussion of public library aims and objectives. See following chapters: 3. 'The reader-centred library'; 4. 'New concepts of service'; 9. 'What are we up to?'; 11. 'The purpose of libraries'.

21 McColvin, L. R., *Theory of book selection for public libraries*, Grafton, 1924. Classic work. Though dated, pages 9 – 84 still worth reading.

22 McColvin, L. R., 'Some administrative aspects of book selection', *Librarian*, **45** (2), Feb. 1956, 21 – 9. Despite its title, gives succinct summary of the fundamentals of book provision for public libraries.

23 McKee, B., *Public libraries – into the 1990's?*, Association of Assistant Librarians, 1987.

24 Spiller, D. J., 'Libraries for all?', *Library Association record*, **90** (4), April 1988, 217 – 18. Plus correspondence on censorship in June, July, August and October issues.

25 Steele, C. (ed.), *Steady state, zero growth and the academic library*, Bingley, 1978. On the 'self-renewing library'.

26 Tucker, P. E., 'The development of research collections in the new university libraries in Britain', *Libri*, **30** (1), March 1980, 66 – 81.

27 UNESCO, *Public library manifesto*, UNESCO, 1973. Statement of public library aims for international consumption.

28 University Grants Committee, *Capital provision for university libraries: report of a working party*, HMSO, 1976.

29 Usherwood, B., *The public library as public knowledge*, Library Association, 1989.

30 Wellard, J. H., *Book selection: its principles and practice*, Grafton, 1937. Dated, but chapters 6, 7, 8 and 9 contain valuable discussion of literary, sociological and administrative approaches to book provision for public libraries.

Chapter 4 Budgeting

31 American Library Association, Resources and Technical Services Division, *Guidelines for the allocation of library materials budgets: working draft*, ALA, 1977.

32 Fletcher, J., 'Financial management systems', in Line, M. B., *Academic library management*, Library Association, 1990, 215–22.

33 Graham, T. W., 'University library finance in the 1980's', in Dyson, B., *The modern academic library*, Library Association, 1989, 32 – 56.

34 Thompson, J. and Carr, R., *University library administration*, Bingley, 4th ed., 1987. Pages 24 – 37 on university finance.

Chapter 5   Users

35 Ayris, P., *The stimulation of creativity: a review of the literature concerning the concept of browsing 1970 – 85*, University of Sheffield Consultancy and Research Unit.

36 Beal, C., *Community profiling for librarians*, Centre for Research on User Studies, University of Sheffield, 1985.

37 Benge, R. C., *Bibliography and the provision of books*, Association of Assistant Librarians, 1963. Pages 91 – 6 on provision and demand.

38 Blagden, J., *Do we really need libraries?*, Bingley, 1980.

39 Bonn, G. S., 'Evaluation of the collection', *Library trends*, January 1974, 265 – 304.

40 Brophy, P. and others, *The effectiveness of library expenditure: investigations into the selection of books and their subsequent use*, Bristol Polytechnic Library, 1985.

41 Buckland, M. K., 'An operational research study of a variable loan and duplication policy at the University of Lancaster', *Library quarterly*, **42**, 1972, 97 – 106.

42 Centre for Library and Information Management, *Reader failure at the shelf*, CLAIM, University of Loughborough, 1982.

43 Corkill, C. and Mann, M., *Information needs in the humanities*, University of Sheffield Centre for Research on User Studies, 1978. (BLR&D report no. 5455).

44 Craghill, D., *Public library user studies: what have we learned and where do we go from here?* Consultancy and Research Unit, Dept. of Information Studies, University of Sheffield, 1988.

45 Ford, G., *Review of methods employed in determining the use of library stock*, BNB Research Fund, 1990.

46 Goodall, D., *Browsing in public libraries*, Dept. of Library and Information Studies, Loughborough University of Technology, 1989.

47 Greenwood, D., 'The BNB Research Fund', *Journal of librarianship*, **21** (4), October 1989, 246 – 59.

48 Harris, C., *Management information systems in library and information services*, Taylor Graham, 1987.

49 Hart, M. and others, *Book selection and use in academic libraries*, Centre for Library and Information Management, 1986.

50 Hatt, F., *The reading process: a framework for analysis and description*, Bingley, 1976.

51 Hindle, A. K. and Buckland, M. K., 'In-library book usage in relation to circulation', *Collection management*, **2** (4), Winter 1978, 265 – 77.

52 Humphries, K. W., 'Survey of borrowing from the main library, the University of Birmingham', *Libri*, **14** (2), 1964, 126 – 35.

53 Jordan, P. and Walley, E., *Learning about the community: a guide for public libraries*, School of Librarianship, Leeds Polytechnic, 1977.

54 Kantor, P. B., *Objective performance measures for academic and research libraries*, Washington: Association of Research Libraries, 1984.

55 Kent, A. L., *Use of library materials: the University of Pittsburgh study*, New York: Dekker, 1979.

56 Lancaster, F. W., 'Evaluating collections by their use', *Collection management*, **4** (1/2), Spring/Summer 1982, 15 – 44.

57 Lancaster, F. W., *If you want to evaluate your library . . .*, Library Association, 1988.

58 Line, M. B., 'The ability of a university library to provide books wanted by researchers', *Journal of librarianship*, **5**, 37 – 41.

59 Line, M. B., *Library surveys: an introduction to their use, planning, procedure and presentation*, Bingley, 2nd ed., 1982.

60 Luckham, B., *The library in society: a study of the public library in an urban setting*, Library Association, 1971.

61 Mansbridge, J., 'Availability studies in libraries', *Library and information science research*, **8** (4), Oct – Dec 1986, 299 – 314.

62 Martyn, J., *Literature searching habits and attitudes of research scientists*, British Library, 1987.

63 Meadows, A. J., *Communication in science*, Butterworth, 1974.

64 Orr, R. H., 'Measuring the goodness of library services: a general framework for considering qualitative measures', *Journal of documentation*, **29** (3), September 1973, 315 – 32.

65 Overton, C. D., *Review of management information from computer-based circulation systems in academic libraries*, British Library, 1979. (BLR&D report no. 5471).

66 Peasgood, A. N., 'Towards demand-led book acquisitions? Experiences in the University of Sussex Library', *Journal of librarianship*, **18** (4), October 1986, 242 – 56.

67 Roberts, N. and Wilson, T. D., 'User studies at Sheffield University', *Journal of librarianship*, **20** (4), October 1988, 270 – 90.

68 Rubin, R., *In-house use of materials in public libraries*, University of Illinois, Graduate School of Librarianship and Information Science, 1986.

69 Schofield, J. L. and others, 'Evaluation of an academic library's stock effectiveness', *Journal of librarianship*, **7**, July 1975, 207 – 27.

70 Skelton, B., 'Scientists and social scientists as information users; a comparison of results of science user studies with the investigation into information requirements of the social sciences', *Journal of librarianship*, **5** (2), April 1973, 138 – 56.

71 Stevens, R. E., 'The use of library materials in doctoral research: a study of the effect of differences in research method', *Library quarterly*, **23** (1), January 1953, 33 – 41.

72 Stone, S. and Harris, C., *Designing a user study: general research design*, Centre for Research on User Studies, University of Sheffield, 1984. Other titles in this series are: 2. *Basic social research techniques*; 3. *Analysing data*; 4. *Writing research reports*; 5. *Questionnaires*; 6. *Interviews*; 7. *Observation*.

73 Totterdell, B. and Bird, J., *The effective library. Report of the Hillingdon project on public library effectiveness*, Library Association, 1976.

74 Vickery, B. C. and others, 'Report by Birmingham University Library on surveys carried out in 1964 on the use of the library by undergraduates, graduate students and staff', in University Grants Committee, *Report of the committee on libraries*, HMSO, 1967, 213 – 28.

75 Wenger, C. B. and Childress, J., 'Journal evaluation in a large research library', *Journal of the American Society for Information Science*, **28** (5), September 1977, 293 – 9.

Chapter 6 Book evaluation

76 Hatt, F., *The reading process: a framework for analysis and description*, Bingley, 1976. Pages 58 – 61 on readability formulae.

77 Jones, A. and Pratt, G., 'The categorisation of adult non-fiction', *Journal of librarianship*, 6 (2), April 1974, 91 – 8.

78 McClellan, A. W., *The logistics of a public library bookstock*, Association of Assistant Librarians, 1978. Pages 65 – 6 'the impact of reservations'; pages 68 – 73 'analysis by level or function of material'; pages 73 – 6 'assessment of readability'.

79 Noble, D. H. and Noble, C. M., 'A survey of book reviews', *Library Association record*, **76** (5), May 1974, 90, 92. (Also separately published, in a fuller version, by Noble and Beck Ltd, 1974.)

80 Roberts, D. H. E., 'An analysis of the request and reservation service of Nottinghamshire County Library', *Journal of librarianship*, **5** (1), January 1973.

81 Sutherland, J. A., *Fiction and the fiction industry*, Athlone Press, 1978. Chapter 5: the reviewing establishment, 84 – 106.

82 Sweeney, Russell, *International target audience code (ITAC): a proposal and report on its development and testing*, IFLA International Office for UBC, 1977.

83 Walford, A. J., *Reviews and reviewing: a guide*, Mansell, 1986.

84 Whittaker, K., *Systematic evaluation: methods and sources for assessing books*, Bingley, 1982.

Chapter 7 Bibliographies

85 Baumfield, B. H., 'Sources for the selection of books and other materials', in Lock, R. N. (ed.), *Manual of library economy*, Bingley, 1977, 159 – 87.

86 Benge, R. C., *Bibliography and the provision of books*, Association of Assistant Librarians, 1963. See pages 153 – 203 on bibliographies.

87 Greenwood, D. (ed.), *Bibliographic records in the book world: needs and capabilities*, BNB Research Fund, 1988. See papers by Butcher, J. E., 'British Library bibliographic services', 104 – 8; Whitaker, D. E., 'The Whitaker approach to bibliographic content', 110 – 16; Bunce, J., 'How major library suppliers can meet the bibliographic needs of users in various library sectors', 96 – 102.

88 Olle, J. G., *A guide to sources of information in libraries*, Gower, 1984. See pages 107 – 64 on bibliographical sources.

89 Whittaker, K., *Systematic evaluation: methods and sources for assessing books*, Bingley, 1982. See pages 116 – 31 on bibliographies.

Chapter 8   Logistics

90 Betts, D. and Hargrave, R., *How many books?* MCB Publications, 1983. Describes logistic applications in the County of Surrey.

91 Buckland, Michael, *Book availability and the library users*, Pergamon, 1975. Summary of the literature of stock logistics, especially in academic libraries. Gives detailed reports of several research projects, including one on short loan collections.

92 Houghton, T., *Bookstock management in public libraries*, Bingley, 1985. See especially sections on bookstock rotation (pages 89 – 101) and stock injection (pages 76 – 88).

93 McClellan, A. W., *The reader, the library and the book*, Bingley, 1973. Chapter 8 (Systematic stock control in public libraries, pages 83 – 105) provides an introduction to the McClellan system.

94 McClellan, A. W., *The logistics of a public library bookstock*, Association of Assistant Librarians, 1978. A full exposition of McClellan's system.

95 Moore, N., 'Systematic bookstock management in public libraries', *Journal of librarianship*, **15** (4), October 1983, 262 – 76.

Chapter 9   Weeding

96 Brown, A. J., 'Some library costs and options', *Journal of librarianship*, **12** (4), October 1980, 211 – 16.

97 Buckland, Michael, *Book availability and the library users*, Pergamon, 1975.

98 Ford, G., 'A review of relegation practice' in Corrall, S., *Collection development: options for effective management*, Taylor Graham, 1988, 71 – 87.

99 Ford, G., 'Stock relegation in some British university libraries', *Journal of libraranship*, **12** (1), January 1980, 42 – 55.

100 Fussler, H. H. and Simon, J. L., *Patterns in the use of books in large research libraries*, University of Chicago Press, 1969. Includes a discussion of weeding principles.

101 Gilder, L. and others, *The relegation and storage of material in academic libraries: a literature review*, Centre for Library and Information Management, University of Loughborough, 1980. Commissioned by the UGC Steering Group on Library Research.

102 Hart, M. and others, *Book selection and use in academic libraries*, Centre for Library and Information Management, 1986.

103 Kirby, I., 'Bookbinding and repairs' in Stoakley, R. (ed.), *After selection*, Library Association, South Western Branch, 1981. By the sales manager of Remploy Book Binding Division.

104 Line, M. B. and Sandison, A., ' "Obsolescence" and changes in the use of literature with time', *Journal of documentation*, **30** (3), September 1974, 283 – 350. The quotation is from page 319.

105 Raffell, J. A. and Shishko, R., *Systematic analysis of university libraries*, MIT Press, 1969. Includes a discussion of weeding principles.

106 Rowley, J. E. and Turner, C. M. C., *The dissemination of information*, Deutsch, 1978. Pages 41 – 5 give a clear summary of recent studies of obsolescence.

107 Slote, Stanley J., *Weeding library collections*, Libraries Unlimited Inc (US), 1975. Includes a descriptive bibliography on the literature of weeding.

108 Taylor, C. and Urquhart, N. C., *Management and assessment of stock control in academic libraries: a report on a research project*, British Library, 1976 (BLR&D report no 5263). The quotation is from page 24.

109 Trueswell, Richard W., 'Determining the optimal number of volumes for a library's core collection', *Libri*, **16**, 1966, 49 – 50.

110 University Grants Committee, *Capital provision for university libraries: report of a working party*, HMSO, 1976 (The Atkinson report). The document which first advocated the principle of the self-renewing university library.

111 Whittaker, K., *Systematic evaluation: methods and sources for evaluating books*, Bingley, 1982. Pages 132 – 8 give some practical advice on weeding.

112 Williams, S. R., 'Weeding an academic library using the Slote method', *British journal of academic librarianship*, **1** (2), Summer 1986, 147 – 59.

Chapter 12   Management

113 Higginbottom, J., 'The subject librarian', in Revill, D. H., *Personnel management in polytechnic libraries*, Gower, 1987, 155 – 74.

114 Higham, N., *The library and the university: observations on a service*, Deutsch, 1980. Pages 36 – 60 on how selection is managed.

115 Hindle, A., *Developing an acquisitions system for a university library*, British Library, 1977 (BLR&D research report no 5351).

116 McClellan, A. W., *The reader, the library and the book: selected papers 1949 – 1970*, Bingley, 1973. See pages 58 – 67 (the organization of a library for subject specialization); pages 68 – 71 (professional work for professional librarians); pages 116 – 23 (a systems approach to libraries).

117 University Grants Committee, *Report of the committee on libraries (the Parry Report)*, HMSO, 1967, 64 – 8.

118 Urquhart, J. A. and Schofield, J. L., 'Overlap of acquisitions in the University of London libraries: a study and a methodology', *Journal of librarianship*, **4** (1), January 1972, 32 – 47.

Chapter 13   Interlending

119 Brown, A. J., 'Some library costs and options', *Journal of librarianship*, **12** (4), October 1980, 211 – 16.

120 Gwinn, N. E. and Mosher, P., 'Co-ordinating collection development: the RLG Conspectus', *College and research libraries*, **44** (2), 1983, 128 – 40.

121 Line, M. B., 'Local acquisitions policies in a national context', in Jeffreys, A. (ed.), *The art of the librarian*, Oriel Press, 1973.

122 Line, M. B., 'Access to collections, including inter-library loans', in Parker, J. S., *Aspects of library development planning*, Mansell, 1983.

123 Plassard, M.-F., 'The impact of new technology on document availability and access', *Interlending and document supply*, **17** (1), January 1989, 3 – 10.
124 White, B., *Interlending in the UK, 1985*, The British Library, 1986.
125 Wilson, T. D. and Masterston, W. A. J., *Local library cooperation*, University of Sheffield Postgraduate School of Library and Information Science, 1974.

Chapter 14 The book trade

126 Astbury, R., 'The book trade', in *British librarianship and information work 1981 – 5 Vol 2*, Library Association, 1988.
127 Baumfield, B. H., *Libraries and the book trade: aspects of interface and cooperation*, MA thesis, Loughborough Univ. of Technology, 1982.
128 Benge, R. C., *Bibliography and the provision of books*, Association of Assistant Librarians, 1963. Pages 116 – 52 on publisher's role from the librarian's viewpoint.
129 Blond, A., *The book book*, Cape, 1985. Entertaining survey of how publishers operate.
130 *The book report 1989*, Euromonitor Publications, 1989. Invaluable statistical surveys of the book world.
131 Capital Planning Information, *Private process/public advantage: the value to public library authorities of special services provided by library suppliers*, BNB Research Fund, 1987.
132 Chapman, L., *Buying books for libraries*, Bingley, 1989. Book on acquisition procedures for British librarians.
133 Curwen, P. J., *The UK publishing industry*, Pergamon, 1981.
134 Greenwood, D. (ed.), *Bibliographic records in the book world: needs and capabilities*, BNB Research Fund, 1988. Especially: Glayzer, J., 'Library selection/acquisition requirements in public libraries', 30 – 4; Peasgood, A. N., 'Acquisition/selection librarians – academic libraries', 38 – 44; Bunce, J., 'How major library suppliers can meet the bibliographic needs of users in various library sectors', 96 – 102.
135 Magrill, R. L. and Hickey, D. J., *Acquisitions management and collection development in libraries*, Acquisition procedures for American librarians. (Formerly *The acquisition of library materials*, by S. Ford.)

136 Mann, P., *From author to reader: a social study of books*, Routledge, 1982.
137 Norrie, I., *Mumby's publishing and bookselling in the twentieth century*, Bell & Hyman, 6th ed., 1980.
138 Oakeshott, P., *Liaison in the book world*, BNB Research Fund, 1986.
139 Pryce, V. and Littlechild, M., *Book prices in the United Kingdom: a study by Peat Marwood McLintock*, BNB Research Fund, 1989.

Chapter 15   Standards
140 Department of Education and Science, Library Advisory Councils, *Public library service points*, HMSO, 1971.
141 Department of Education and Science, *Standards of public library service in England and Wales (the Bourdillon Report)*, HMSO, 1962.
142 International Federation of Library Associations, *Standards for public libraries*, Verlag Dokumentat, 2nd ed., 1978.
143 Sewell, P., 'Standards, norms and targets: problems of international comparison', in Parker, J. S., *Aspects of library development planning*, Mansell, 1983.
144 *Standards of the public library service in Scotland. Report by a working party appointed by the Arts and Recreation Committee of the Convention of Scottish Library Associations*, COSLA, 1986.
145 University Grants Committee, *Report of the Committee on Libraries (the Parry Report)*, HMSO, 1967.
146 Withers, F. N., *Standards for library service: an international survey*, UNESCO Press, 1974.

Chapter 16   Periodicals
147 Blake, M. and Meadows, A. J., 'Journals at risk', *Journal of librarianship*, **16** (2), April 1984, 118 – 28.
148 Buckland, Michael, *Book availability and the library users*, Pergamon, 1975. Pages 17 – 30 discuss the relegation of journals.
149 Clarke, A., 'The use of serials at the British Library Lending Division, 1980', *Interlending review*, **9** (4), 1981, 111 – 17.
150 Davinson, Donald, *The periodicals collection*, 2nd ed. Deutsch, 1978. See especially Chapter 11 (acquisitions policy), 161 – 76.

151 Fussler, H. H. and Simon, J. L., *Patterns in the use of books in large research libraries*, University of Chicago Press, 1969. Despite its title, the work also surveys periodical provision.

152 Huff, William H., 'The acquisition of serial publications', *Library trends*, **18** (3), January 1970, 254 – 317.

153 Houghton, B. and Prosser, C., 'Rationalization of serial holdings in special libraries', *Aslib proceedings*, **26** (6), June 1974, 223 – 35.

154 Kefford, B. and Line, M. B., 'Core collections of journals for national interlending purposes', *Interlending review*, **10** (2), 1982, 35 – 43.

155 Kent, A., *Use of library material: the University of Pittsburgh study*, Dekker, 1979.

156 Lancaster, F. W., *If you want to evaluate your library* . . . , Library Association, 1988. Pages 60 – 71 on the evaluation of periodicals.

157 Line, M. B. and Sandison, A., "Obsolescence" and changes in the use of literature with time', *Journal of documentation*, **30** (3), September 1974.

158 Line, M. B., 'Changes in rank lists of serials over time: interlending vs citation data', *Interlending and document supply*, **12** (4), October 1984, 145 – 7.

159 Meadows, A. J., *Communication in science*, Butterworths, 1974, 152 – 71. On the scatter of scientific literature.

160 Oldman, C. M. and Davinson, D., *The usage of periodicals in public libraries: an investigation carried out in 1972 – 3*, Leeds Polytechnic Department of Librarianship, 1975.

161 Osborn, A. D., *Serials publications: their place and treatment in libraries*, American Library Association, 1980, 77 – 99. This section is on the principles of serial selection.

162 Rowley, J. G. and Turner, C. M. D., *The dissemination of information*, Deutsch, 1978, 28 – 41. This section on bibliometrics.

163 Scales, P. A., 'Citation analyses as indicators of the use of serials: a comparison of ranked title lists by citation counting and from use data', *Journal of documentation*, **32** (1), 1976, 17 – 25.

164 Taylor, C. and Urquhart, N. C., *Management and assessment of stock control in academic libraries: a report on a research project*, British Library, 1976. (BLR&D report no. 5263).

165 Wood, C. M., 'International exchange between British and Soviet libraries: the managerial problems of acquisition by exchange', *Solanus*, **17**, August 1982, 32 – 43.

166 Woodward, H., 'Journal acquisition versus article acquisition', pages 111 – 17; and Horwill, C., 'Periodicals reviewing by voting', pages 102 – 10; in Corrall, S. (ed.), *Collection development: options for effective management*, Proceedings of a conference of the Library and Information Research Group, University of Sheffield, 1987, Taylor Graham, 1988.

Chapter 17   Foreign language materials

167 Bloomfield, B. C., *Acquisition and provision of foreign books by national and university libraries in the UK*, Mansell, 1972. See especially the section by Maurice Line, 'The national organisation of the acquisition of foreign books: a personal view', 201 – 11.

168 Clough, Eric and Quarmby, J., *A public library service for ethnic minorities in Great Britain*, Library Association, 1978.

169 Dixon, J. (ed.), *Fiction in libraries*, Library Association, 1986, 93 – 103 (section on foreign fiction by P. Marcan).

170 Elliott, P., *Public libraries and self-help ethnic minority organizations*, Polytechnic of North London, School of Librarianship and Information Studies, 1984.

171 Elliott, P., *Access to ethnic minority materials*, Polytechnic of North London, School of Librarianship and Information Studies, 1986.

172 Ellen, Sandra R., 'Survey of foreign language problems facing the research worker', *Interlending review*, **7** (2), April 1979.

173 Hutchins, W. J. and others, *The language barrier: a study in depth of foreign language methods in the research activity of an academic community*, University of Sheffield Postgraduate School of Librarianship and Information Science, 1971.

Chapter 18   Out-of-print books

174 Cameron, K. J. and Roberts, M., 'Desiderata file maintenance: purging and its policies', *Journal of librarianship*, **14** (2), April 1982.

175 Cave, Roderick, *Rare book librarianship*, Bingley, 2nd ed., 1982.
176 Cox, D., 'Rare books and special collections' in Stirling, J. F. (ed.), *University librarianship*, Library Association, 1981 (Handbooks on library practice), 83 – 101.

Chapter 19   Paperbacks

177 Harrison, K. M., *Paperback books in public libraries*, MA dissertation, Department of Library and Information Studies, Loughborough University of Technology, 1984.
178 Hart, M. (ed.), *The use of paperbacks in public libraries in the UK: a review of research*, Centre for Library and Information Management, University of Loughborough, 1983.

Chapter 20   Fiction

179 Atkinson, F., *Fiction librarianship*, Bingley, 1981.
180 Betts, D. A., *Borrowing and the fiction reader*, Library Association, Branch and Mobile Libraries Group, 1987.
181 Dixon, J. (ed.), *Fiction in libraries*, Library Association, 1986. See especially, genre fiction 21 – 111; categorization 162 – 6.
182 Goodall, D., *Browsing in public libraries*, Department of Library and Information Studies, Loughborough University of Technology, 1989.
183 Leavis, Q. D., *Fiction and the reading public*, Chatto & Windus, 1932. Study of reading tastes in 19th and 20th centuries.
184 McCleish, K., *Bloomsbury good reading guide*, Bloomsbury Press, 1989. Guide to fiction authors which links writers similar in style or content.
185 McClellan, A. W., 'The reading dimension in effectiveness and service', *Library review*, **30**, Summer 1981, 77 – 86. Strong argument for taking fiction provision seriously.
186 Mann, P. H., *Books: buyers and borrowers*, Deutsch, 1971. Study by sociologist.
187 Mann, P. H., *A new survey: the facts about romantic fiction*, Mills & Boon, 1974.
188 Mann, P. H., *Reader's guide to fiction authors*, Centre for Library and Information Management, 1985. Similar approach to McLeish title above.

189 Olle, J. G., 'Fiction – the missing service', *New library world*, **82** (972), June 1981, 101 – 4.

190 Pejtersen, A. M., 'Fiction and library classification', *Scandinavian public library quarterly*, 11 (1), 1978, 5 – 12.

191 Sear, L. and Jennings, B., *How readers select fiction*, Kent County Council, 1986.

192 Sear, L. and Jennings, B., *Novel ideas: a browsing area for fiction*, Kent County Council, 1989.

193 Spiller, D. J., *The provision of fiction for public libraries*, MLS dissertation, Loughborough University of Technology, 1979. Includes studies of fiction reviews, and the management of fiction provision in 12 public library authorities.

194 Spiller, D. J., 'The provision of fiction for public libraries', *Journal of librarianship*, **12** (4), October 1980, 238 – 66. Survey of fiction use in four libraries.

195 Sumsion, J., *PLR in practice*, Registrar of Public Lending Right, 1988. Overview of Public Lending Right statistics. See also review by Betts, D. A., *Journal of librarianship*, **21** (1), Jan. 1989, 62 – 9.

196 Sutherland, J. A., *Fiction and the fiction industry*, Athlone Press, 1978. Study of fiction publishing.

197 Whatley, H. A., 'Fiction – the missing service', *Librarian*, **45** (6), July 1956, 109 – 14. Imaginative plea for fiction provision to be taken more seriously by librarians, still relevant 30 years after publication.

198 Williams, R., *Communications*, Penguin, 3rd ed., 1976. Pages 109 – 16 on high culture and mass culture.

Chapter 21   Biography

199 Ainley, P. and Totterdell, B., *Alternative arrangement: new approaches to public library stock*, Association of Assistant Librarians, 1982.

200 McClellan, A. W., *The reader, the library and the book: selected papers 1949 – 1970*, Bingley, 1973. Chapter 3 'The reader centred library'.

201 Quinton, Lord, 'The cultural value of books', *Library Association record*, **91** (11), November 1989, 645 – 51.

202 Spiller, D. J, 'A strategy for biography provision in public libraries', *Library review*, **37** (1), 1988, 40 – 4.

Chapter 22   Audiovisual materials

203 American Library Association, *Guidelines for audio-visual materials and services for large public libraries*, ALA, 1975.

204 Asheim, L., ' "Introduction" to conference proceedings on the selection of non-book materials', *Library quarterly*, **45** (1), January 1975.

205 *Bibliographical control of audio-visual materials*, Proceedings of a seminar organized by the Council for Educational Technology and the Library Association, 13 November 1985, Library Association Audiovisual Group, 1987.

206 British Library, 'The British Library and non-book materials: a statement', *Audiovisual librarian*, **9** (4), Autumn 1983, 183 – 92.

207 Fothergill, R. and Butchart, I., *Non-book materials in libraries: a practical guide*, Bingley, 2nd ed., 1984. Pages 159 – 96 on selection.

208 Heery, M. J., 'Audiovisual materials in academic libraries: preliminary report of a survey conducted on behalf of the Library Association Audiovisual Group', *Audiovisual librarian*, **9** (4), Autumn 1983, 183 – 92.

209 Miller, P., *The production and bibliographical control of non-book materials in the UK: final report*, Polytechnic of North London, 1985.

210 Pinion, C. F., *Legal deposit of non-book materials: a consideration of the practical problems, with reference to alternative methods of collection*, British Library, 1986.

211 Pinion, C. F., 'Audiovisual materials', in *British librarianship and information work 1981 – 5 Vol 2*, Library Association, 1988, 142 – 55.

212 Roberts, M., *The use of audio-visual materials by individual subject departments within a university and the development of library services*, University of Sheffield, Postgraduate School of Librarianship and Information Science, 1975.

Sound recordings

213 Saddington, G. H. and Cooper, E., 'Audio cassettes as library materials: an introduction', *Audiovisual librarian*, 2nd ed., 1984.

Films and videos

214 Butcher, J., 'Video supply in libraries', *Audiovisual librarian*, **13** (2), May 1987, 80 – 7.

215 Harrison, H. P., *Film library techniques*, Focal Press, 1973. See pages 31 – 49 on selection.

216 Pinion, C. F., 'Video home lending services in public libraries', *Audiovisual librarian*, **9** (1), Winter 1983, 18 – 23.

217 Udwin, M., 'The problems of video in public libraries', *Audiovisual librarian*, **9** (1), Winter 1983, 24 – 7.

Pictures

218 British Library, *Report of the working party on the provision of materials for the study of art*, British Library, 1983.

219 Evans, H. and Evans, M., *Picture researcher's handbook*, Van Nostrand, 4th ed., 1989.

220 Evans, H., *Picture librarianship*, Bingley, 1980. Pages 23 – 38 on acquisition.

221 Harrison, H., *Picture librarianship*, Library Association, 1981. Pages 55 – 64 on selection.

222 Pacey, P., *Art library manual*, Bowker, 1977. Chapters by Pacey, P., 'Slides and film-strips', 272 – 84, and Sunderland, J., 'Photographs and reproductions of works of art', 285 – 97.

223 Shaw, R. V., 'Picture professionalism. Part 1', *Special libraries*, **65** (10 & 11), October/November 1974, 421 – 9. On the selection of photographs.

Microforms

224 Ashby, P., *Microform publishing*, Butterworth, 1979.

225 Grimshaw, A., 'Microforms in libraries', in *British librarianship and information work 1981 – 5 Vol 2*, Library Association, 1988, 132 – 41.

226 Teague, S. J., *Microform, video and electronic librarianship*, Butterworth, 2nd ed., 1985.

Computer software

227 Dolphin, P., 'Computer software as library materials', *Audiovisual librarian*, **11** (7), Summer 1985, 168 – 71.

228 Ebrahim, H., 'Bedfordshire County Library microcomputer project', *Program*, **19** (2), April 1985, 150 – 9.

229 Fielden, D., 'Buying software: a customer survival kit', *Audiovisual librarian*, **13** (1), February 1987, 50 – 3.

230 Skinner, H., 'Microcomputer software in libraries', *Audiovisual librarian*, **13** (4), Autumn 1987, 200 – 8.

231 Tage, W. and Templeton, R., *Computer software: finding it and supplying it*, British Library, 1983.

Chapter 23   Databases

232 Clarke, J. E., *A review of parallel publishing*, British Library, 1989.

233 Foster, A., *Which data base? an evaluative guide to on-line bibliographic data bases in business and the social sciences*, Headland Press, 1981.

234 Houghton, B. and Wisdom, J. C., *Non-bibliographic on-line data bases: an investigation into their uses within the fields of economics and business studies*, British Library, 1981.

235 Large, J. A., 'Evaluating on-line and CD-ROM reference sources', *Journal of librarianship,* **21** (2), April 1989, 87 – 108.

236 Royce, C. and others, *CD-ROM: usage and prospects*, British Library, 1989.

References

237 Association of College and Research Libraries, *Standards for college libraries*, ACRL, 1986.

238 Association of Research Libraries and Association of College and Research Libraries, *Standards of university libraries*, Chicago: Association of College and Research Libraries, 1979.

239 *Audiovisual librarian*, **4** (1), Summer 1977.

240 *Average prices of British academic books*, Library and Information Statistics Unit, Dept. of Library and Information Studies, Loughborough University of Technology. Six-monthly.

241 Benge, R. C., *Bibliography and the provision of books*, Association of Assistant Librarians, 1963, 95.

242 Benge, R. C., *Libraries and cultural change*, Bingley, 1970, 99.

243 Bishop, J. and Lewis, P. R., 'Blaise-line and the British national bibliography: profiles of users and uses', *Journal of librarianship*, **17** (2), April 1985, 119 – 36.

244 Blackwells Periodical Division, Information on periodical prices produced annually, and published (customarily in May issue) in the *Library Association record*.

245 Blond, A., *The book book*, Cape, 1985, 138 – 9.

246 Blond, A., *The publishing game*, Cape, 1971, 43.

247 Blond, A., op. cit., 58 – 9.

248 *Book auction records*, Stevens and Stiles, annual. *American book prices current*, New York: Bancroft, Parkman, annual. *Bookman's price index*, Gale Research Company, annual.

249 *Book review index*, Detroit: Gale Research Company. Six issues p.a.

250 *British Library Act*, HMSO, 1972.

251 Bryant, P., 'The use of cataloguing-in-publication in United Kingdom libraries', *Journal of librarianship*, **15** (1), January 1983, 1 – 18.

252 Budd, J. M., 'Allocation formulas in practice', *Library acquisitions: practice and theory*, **13** (4), 1989, 381 – 90.

253 Canadian Association of College and University Libraries, *Guide to Canadian university library standards*, Ottawa, 1964.

254 *Cassell's directory of publishing*, Cassell, every two years.

255 Centre for Interfirm Comparisons, *Inter-library comparisons in academic libraries*, British Library, 1984.

256 Chartered Institute of Public Finance and Accountancy, *Public library statistics. Actuals. Estimates*, CIPFA. (Both annual.)

257 Cropper, B., *Going soft: some uses of paperbacks in libraries*, Branch and Mobile Libraries Group of the Library Association, 1986.

258 Diodata, L. W. and Diodata, V. P., 'The use of gifts in a medium sized university library', *Collection management*, **5** (1/2), Spring/Summer 1983, 53 – 71.

259 Evans, G. E., 'Book selection and book collection usage in academic libraries', *Library quarterly*, **40** (3), July 1970, 297 – 308.

260 Ford, G., *Review of methods employed in determining the use of library stock*, BNB Research Fund, 1990, 37 – 8.

261 Ford, G., op. cit., 47 – 8.

262 Ford, S., *The acquisition of library materials*, American Library Association, 1973.

263 Grogan, D., *Science and technology: an introduction to the literature*, Bingley, 4th ed., 1982, 118.

264 Harris, C., 'A comparison of issues and in-library use of books', *Aslib proceedings*, **29** (3), March 1977, 118 – 26.

265 Heaney, H., 'Networking and interlending in the United Kingdom', *Interlending and document supply*, **17** (2), April 1989, 46 – 8.

266 Houghton, B. and Prosser, C., 'Survey of the opinions of BLLD users in special libraries and the effects of non-immediate access to journals', *Aslib proceedings*, **26** (9), September 1974.

267 Houghton, T., *Bookstock management in public libraries*, Bingley, 1985, 71.

268 International Federation of Library Associations, *Standards for public libraries*, IFLA, 1973.

269 Jones, A., 'Criteria for evaluation of public library services', *Journal of librarianship*, **2** (4), October 1970, 118 – 245.

270 Kantor, P. B., 'Availability analysis', *Journal of the American Society for Information Science*, **27** (5), Sept/Oct 1976, 311 – 19.
271 Lancaster, F. W., *If you want to evaluate your library* . . . , Library Association, 1988, 67.
272 Lancaster, F. W., *The measurement and evaluation of library services*, Information Resources Press, 1977, vii.
273 Luckham, B., *The library in society: a study of the public library in an urban setting*, Library Association, 1971, table 46.
274 Luckham, B., op. cit., 62 (table 40).
275 McClellan, A. W., *The logistics of a public library book-stock*, Association of Assistant Librarians, 1978, 86 – 7.
276 McClellan, A. W., op. cit., 40 – 50.
277 McClellan, A. W., op. cit., 57.
278 McClellan, A. W., op. cit., 51 – 7.
279 McClellan, A. W., op. cit., 68 – 72.
280 McClellan, A. W., op. cit., 54 – 5.
281 McClellan, A. W., op. cit., 27 – 8.
282 McClellan, A. W., *The reader, the library and the book*, Bingley, 1973, 83.
283 McClellan, A. W., op. cit., 45.
284 McClellan, A. W., op. cit., 48.
285 McClellan, A. W., op. cit., 84 – 5.
286 McClellan, A. W., op. cit., 89 – 91.
287 McClellan, A. W., op. cit., 94 – 6.
288 McColvin, L. R., *The public library service: its post war reorganisation and development*, Library Association, 1943.
289 Mann, P. H., *Books: buyers and borrowers*, Deutsch, 1971, 8.
290 *The new public libraries: integration and innovation*, Papers delivered at the 1972 Weekend School of the County Libraries Group of the Library Association, Library Association, 1972, 67.
291 Oakeshott, P., *Trends in journal subscriptions*, Publishers Association, 1987.
292 Payne, G. and Willers, J., 'Using management information in a polytechnic library', *Journal of librarianship*, **21** (1), January 1989, 19 – 35.
293 Penna, C. V. and others, *National library and information services*, Butterworths, 1971, 100 – 2.
294 Public Libraries and Museums Act, HMSO, 1964.

295 *Public libraries in Australia: report of a committee of inquiry into public libraries*, Canberra: Government Printer of Australia, 1976.
296 Ranganathan, S. R., *Library book selection*, 2nd ed., Asia Publishing House, 1966, 95.
297 Ranganathan, S. R., op. cit.
298 Revill, D. H., 'Availability as a performance measure', *Journal of librarianship*, **19** (1), January 1987, 16 – 30.
299 Revill, D. H., 'An availability study in cooperation with a school of librarianship and information studies', *Library review*, **37** (1), 1988, 17 – 34.
300 Robert, N. and Bull, G., 'Professional education and practice: a survey of past students. (MA Information Studies and Social Sciences) of the Postgraduate School of Librarianship and Information Science, University of Sheffield 1973/4 to 1979/80', *Journal of librarianship*, **15** (1), January 1983, 29 – 46.
301 Smith, M., 'Book selection sources', *Library Association record*, **81** (3), March 1979, 31.
302 Spiller, D. J., *The provision of fiction for public libraries*, MLS dissertation, Loughborough University of Technology, 1979, 40.
303 *Statistical approaches to stock management: measures of current performance in Hertfordshire*, Hertfordshire Library Service, 1984.
304 *Stock relegation in practice in major academic libraries in N E England*, Library Association, Universities Section, 1982.
305 Thompson, A. H., 'Relationships between academic libraries and audio-visual production services – the facts. Part 1', *Audiovisual librarian*, **14** (3), August 1988, 136 – 41.
306 Totterdell, B. and Bird, J., *The effective library. Report of the Hillingdon project on public library effectiveness*, Library Association, 1976, 130.
307 Trueswell, R. W., 'Some behavioural patterns of library users: the 80/20 rule', *Wilson library bulletin*, **43** (5), January 1969, 458 – 61.
308 Turner, S. E., *A survey of borrowers' reactions to literary fiction in Beeston Library, Nottinghamshire*, MA dissertation, Dept. of Library and Information Studies, Loughborough University of Technology, 1987.
309 Walford, A. J., *Guide to reference material 3 vols.*, Library Association, 1989, 1982, 1987.

310 Williams, G., *Library cost models: owning versus borrowing serial publications*, Office of Science Information Service, National Science Foundation (US), 1968.
311 Woodhead, P. A. and Martin, J. V., 'Subject specialization in British university libraries: a survey', *Journal of librarianship*, **14** (2), April 1982.
312 Woodward, A. M., *Factors affecting the renewal of periodical subscriptions: a study of decision making in libraries with special reference to economics and inter-library lending*, Aslib, 1978.
313 *Writers' and artists' yearbook*, A. and C. Black, annual.

Index

210

213